END OF THE EARTH

END OF THE EARTH

Voyages to Antarctica

PETER MATTHIESSEN

NATIONAL GEOGRAPHIC
WASHINGTON, D.C.

END OF THE EARTH

TWO VOYAGES

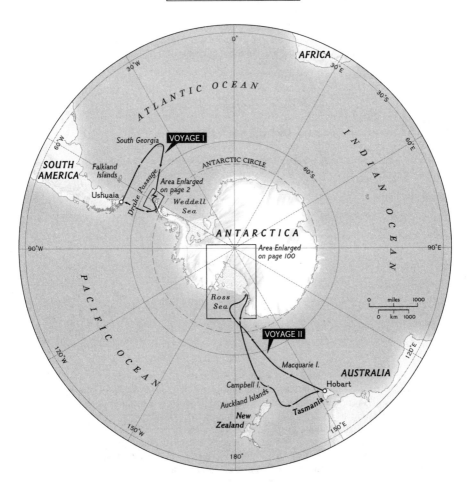

Published by the National Geographic Society

Photographs by Birgit Freybe Bateman

First printing, September 2003

Library of Congress Cataloging-in-Publication Data

Matthiessen, Peter.
 End of the earth : voyages to the White Continent / Peter Matthiessen.
 p. cm.
 ISBN 0-7922-5059-1
 1. Emperor penguin--Antarctica--Antarctic Peninsula. 2. Zoology--Antarctica--Antarctic Peninsula. 3. Matthiessen, Peter--Journeys--Antarctica--Antarctic Peninsula. I. Title.

QL696.S473M375.2003
508.98'9--dc21

2003051254

Interior design by Melissa Farris

Printed in U.S.A.

To My Fine-Feathered Friends
and Excellent Shipmates
on Polar Journeys
North and South:
Victor Emmanuel
Birgit and Bob Bateman

And My As Ever Dear Wife, Maria
Who Has Had to Put Up with Many Years
of Long Absences (Not to Speak of
the Grave Inconvenience of My Presences)
and Has Done So with a
Great and Generous Spirit for
Which I Shall Always Be Grateful.

CONTENTS

Glittering white, shining blue, raven black,
in the light of the sun the land looks like a fairy tale.
Pinnacle after pinnacle, peak after peak,
crevassed, wild as any land on our globe,
it lies, unseen and untrodden.
—ROALD AMUNDSEN

We all have our White South.
—ERNEST SHACKLETON

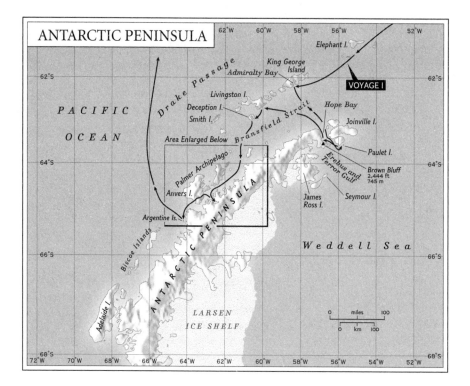

ANTARCTIC PENINSULA

PACIFIC OCEAN

Drake Passage

Elephant I.

King George Island

Admiralty Bay

VOYAGE I

Livingston I.

Deception I.

Smith I.

Hope Bay

Joinville I.

Area Enlarged Below

Bransfield Strait

Palmer Archipelago

Anvers I.

Paulet I.

Erebus and Terror Gulf

Brown Bluff 2,444 ft 745 m

Argentine Is.

James Ross I.

Seymour I.

Biscoe Islands

ANTARCTIC PENINSULA

Weddell Sea

Adelaide I.

LARSEN ICE SHELF

miles 100

km 100

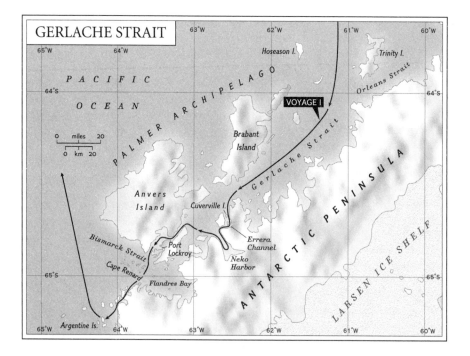

GERLACHE STRAIT

PACIFIC OCEAN

Hoseason I.

Trinity I.

PALMER ARCHIPELAGO

Orleans Strait

VOYAGE I

Brabant Island

miles 20

km 20

Gerlache Strait

Anvers Island

Cuverville I.

ANTARCTIC PENINSULA

Bismarck Strait

Port Lockroy

Errera Channel

Neko Harbor

Cape Renard

Flandres Bay

LARSEN ICE SHELF

Argentine Is.

part one

WIND FALLING
FROM A HIGHER PLACE

TIERRA DEL FUEGO

Four decades ago, exploring backcountry South America, I fetched up in Punta Arenas, Argentina, from where a small ferry crossed the Magellan Straits to Porvenir in Chile. Traveling alone and light, I found cramped space in the back of a crowded truck full of *futbol* fans, crossing the Argentine border on rough, dusty roads to Rio Grande, on the Atlantic coast. From there I hitched a ride south to Ushuaia—"the Water That Pierces the Sunset," as the indigenous Yahgan called the westward waterway through steep forested mountains that is known today as the Beagle Channel.

The frontier settlement at Ushuaia, a small fishing port under precipitous dark peaks, called itself *El Fino del Mundo*, the southernmost settlement on Earth. At Ushuaia, I was accommodated on the floor of the manager's cubby in its lone hotel, the Gran Parque. Terrifying accounts of "rounding the Horn" in the great sailing voyages and whaling expeditions into the southern oceans, had made Cape Horn a destination of my imagination since boyhood, and the next days were spent searching in vain for a boatman who might take me the last 90-odd miles south down wild, dark, uninhabited channels to Cabo de Hornos at the south tip of the New World. For decades afterward, my misty image of what Cape Horn might look and sound like from the sea—the rumbling rocks in the howling gales and wind-ripped explosions of surf—would haunt the back attics of my mind.

In the summer of 1965, living in Galway, I mostly inhabited a book entitled *The Worst Journey in the World,* an account of Robert Falcon Scott's last expedition south from the Ross Sea by a participant, Apsley Cherry-Garrard, the finest book ever written about Antarctic exploration as well as a great literary classic. One day that summer I emerged from "the ice" long enough to discover that the names of two unpromising steeds competing in the famous Galway Races were Ross Sea and Antarctic Sea (and furthermore that Ross Sea would be ridden by an Australian jockey unknown to Irish bettors but well known to me from grand old days at the Neuilly track in Paris as a habitual rider of long-shot horses who triumphed with peculiar regularity against all odds). Off I went on a glorious Irish day to bet much more than was prudent on Ross Sea to win and Antarctic Sea to place. When both of these long shots came through, I stuffed my pockets and went home to my village pub, where I offered dark ale and Irish whiskey to the swiftly assembling clientele. All my new friends were happy to acknowledge that my stars were in order and my destinations preordained and were only too glad to toast my resolve to visit the white continent and behold the mighty emperor of all the penguins.

Thus the Antarctic had joined Cape Horn in a galaxy of Southern Ocean destinations, to which South Georgia, twelve hundred miles east of Cape Horn in the South Atlantic, would be added not long thereafter. That remote high island of glaciers and snow mountains, home to myriad seabirds and marine mammals, is one of the great wildlife spectacles on Earth; it was also the scene of departure and return for the polar explorer Ernest Shackleton of the *Endurance.*

Forty years ago, however, a journey to South Georgia, far less Antarctica, was impossible without an oceangoing vessel and a full-fledged expedition, while a voyage deep into the Ross Sea ice that might arrive early enough to see the emperor penguin before its breeding colonies dispersed would require nothing less than a polar icebreaker.

Since the mid-seventies, I have served as a part-time field leader for a wildlife safari company out of Austin, Texas, which traveled to remote wild places the world over. But only in the last decade, when cruise ship voyages to cold destinations became oddly popular, has limited Antarctic Sea travel become available. By the late nineties, our company was leasing ships to take its birding clients into southern waters, which permitted me to make extended journeys to Antarctica from Tierra del Fuego, and a few years later from Tasmania.

In January 1998, I returned to Ushuaia as a field leader on a wildlife expedition sailing to South Georgia. From there our ship would proceed southwest to the South Shetlands and the northern arm of West Antarctica known as the Antarctic Peninsula, voyaging south along the Peninsula's Pacific coast. Returning north to Tierra del Fuego, she would make her first landfall at Cape Horn, or so I hoped. In these latitudes of storm and shrouding fogs, my chances of seeing the Horn at last were as unpredictable as Fuegian weather.

USHUAIA TODAY, though still a fishing port, is also a town of 57,000 population with a modern airport, and glossy hotels have replaced the old Gran Parque, which perished of old age two years ago and has been torn down. Though the town has crept a mile along the harbor front and is climbing the steep forest slopes toward the small glacier in a cirque of the Martial Peaks, it still seems overwhelmed by Mount Olivia and the five black spires called Cinco Hermanos, thrusting up from the cold mercurial silvers of the Beagle Channel.

In the late afternoon of the sailing date, a triumphal double rainbow forms over the channel, the colors of both arcs glowing in the raining sunlight. One broad band arches over Mount Olivia while the massive column of the other plunges straight into the channel not a mile offshore, igniting the dark surface in a rainbow fire.

ON JANUARY 20, 1998, our ship sails at 6 p.m., due east down the Beagle Channel. The steep coasts to north and south—the emergent ridges of drowned mountains—are forested, forbidding, showing no light or other sign of human habitation. To judge from such place names as Mount Misery and Cape Deceit, Last Hope Bay and Fury Island, the relentless wind and surly weather of these latitudes filled the early voyagers with foreboding and despair.

Seen in cold dusk, in wind and rain, these forest walls have changed little since H.M.S. *Beagle* first appeared in December 1832, bearing Captain Fitzroy and Mr. Darwin to Patagonia and the Galápagos on their epochal voyage of geographical and biological discovery. Charles Darwin (who wrote the first ethnographic description of the region) was appalled by the near-naked Yahgan (the Alacaluf, farther west, at least wore seal skins), who lived mostly in log dugouts and subsisted on shellfish, carrion, and fungus, eked out on occasion, it was said, with the stringy person of some old tribal person. His poor opinion of the native Fuegians was shared by the early settlers, who killed them with imported diseases and all manner of bodily harm. In the 80 years after Darwin's visit, an aboriginal population of about 10,000 was reduced to some 360 souls.[1]

On the lightless coast off our port bow, the white gleams are big male kelp geese. With ornithologist Victor Emanuel, I observe dark strings of cormorant—the blue-eyed cormorant and the rock shag—beating away across the channel. A coven of hulking giant-petrels gathers in a flopping circle around a young Magellanic penguin they have chased to exhaustion in the open water; the vulturish birds mantle long dark wings over their prey as they pick and peck. This small penguin with a dark band crossing its white breast is one of four species of so-called banded penguins, northernmost group among 17 penguin species, which shares the misfortune of living too close to man. The other three are the closely related African or jackass penguin of southern Africa, the Humboldt of South America's west coast, and the Galápagos penguin, which the cold Peru Current (formerly Humboldt Current) has permitted to live as far north as the Equator.[2]

Victor is my excellent friend and longtime associate, a Harvard graduate who in 1973 gave up a successful career as a campaign manager for politicians to found the nature safari company that has leased this research vessel for our expedition. In the past 20 years, with friends and clients and without, we have observed wildlife together on every continent except Antarctica. Victor is an inspired teacher who will discourse eloquently on birds at a moment's notice. In his pursuit of fresh awareness and appreciation of wild things, this slight, bird-quick man has become a sort of ornithological Zen master. "Birds call us into the moment," Victor says.

Toward dark, the ship passes the rusty hull of a dead freighter on a shoal—the last hazard to outward bound mariners, it seems, since the engines slow and the harbor pilot is returned to his own craft. Where the steep coasts open out on the ocean horizon and the last light glints on windy seas of the Drake Passage, a black-browed albatross appears out of the east. This beautiful white species with the quizzical arched brow is the most widespread and abundant of its family.

Already a soft swell tries the hull. A gray-headed albatross comes and goes, planing away across the ghostly wake. To the north lies Isla de los Estados ("Staten Island"), a seagirt mountain ridge so rugged that a landing place might be as difficult to discover as a sensible reason to land. The island ends at Punta Pájaro (Bird Point)—easternmost land's end in Tierra del Fuego. Here the Andes sink beneath the sea. Due east, there is no more land for a thousand miles, in the soaring snow peaks of the island of South Georgia.

CAPE HORN DRIFT

Night falls as the dark land disappears. In the wash of seas along the hull, the ship's diesel engines are oddly quiet, with only small vibration. Not until near midnight come the first hard bang and shudder of the hull's adjustment to the open ocean. She is already well south of those stormy latitudes known to mariners as the "Roaring Forties," having entered the "Furious Fifties," said to be worse.

The R/V *Akademik Ioffe* [3] is a hydro-acoustical research vessel built in Finland in 1989, and based in Kaliningrad, on the Baltic Sea; white and fresh-painted, she might be taken for a small cruise ship were it not for the large scientific and acoustical apparatus on her topmost decks. Pending the recovery of Russia's economy and sufficient funding for her oceanographic work, this ship and others have been leased to foreign companies. [4] The *Ioffe*, at 462 tons, is 117.1 meters long (384 feet), 18.2 meters (60 feet) in beam, with a draft of 5.9 meters (19 feet) and a reinforced steel hull to withstand pack ice up to 1 meter (3.3 feet) thick. Though not an icebreaker, she is classed as an "ice-hardened" vessel worthy of the mighty Southern Ocean.

In addition to 52 in crew, the *Ioffe* has 9 on her ship's staff (including a geologist and a biologist), and also an expedition staff, including, besides Victor and me, the eminent Canadian wildlife artist Robert Bateman, accompanied by his wife, Birgit, a German-born artist-photographer, and also two other field leaders for Victor's company, Greg Lasley of Texas and Brad Schram of California. Like the Batemans, Lasley and Schram are devoted wildlife photographers. Tall, bearded Greg worked as a policeman before making a profession of his passionate hobby of field birding and photography, while Brad is a recognized authority on the birds of southern California. Both will spend hours on the bow, where the wind-sailed birds soar past throughout the day.

WHEN DAYBREAK OPENS the horizon at 5:30, our ship is out of sight of land, lifting and plunging in the toiling iron seas of the Cape Horn Drift that flows east-northeast toward the Falkland Islands. With 12-knot engine speed and a 42-knot following wind, she makes good time.

The gulls and terns seen on the coast have been replaced by ocean wanderers, which glide and dip over the rolling seascapes on long, pointed wings. Almost all of these pelagic species, from the immense wandering albatross to the diminutive storm-petrels, belong to the avian order Procellariiformes (from the Latin *procella*, for storm or gale),[5] which mostly depend on ocean wind for efficient travel: The gale birds include, besides the albatrosses, the shearwaters and petrels, fulmars, diving-petrels, storm-petrels, and giant-petrels. Unlike most of their relatives, the large heavy-bodied giant petrels, known to old-time mariners as "Nellies" or "stinkers," are drawn to the ship's offal (they will find none on this environmentally conscious voyage); the stinkers gyre tirelessly from bow to stern most of the day.

Arching down the ocean sky to vanish behind waves, curving high again like a hurled white cross, our first wandering albatross excites cries of wonder. "I now belong to a higher cult of mortals, for I have seen the Albatross," wrote Dr. Robert Cushman Murphy, whose *Oceanic Birds of South America* (1936) first awakened my interest in these mythic birds and also a longing to visit the breeding colonies on South Georgia, a citadel of peaks and glaciers thrust up out of the blue emptiness, a thousand miles from the nearest continent. "One of the world's most glorious spectacles—like the Alps in mid-ocean," Dr. Murphy called it, enthralled by its majesty as well as its astonishing abundance of marine birds and mammals.

Diomedea exulans, with the longest wingspan (11 feet) of any bird on Earth, is crisscrossed in its ocean arcs by the similar only slightly smaller royal albatross. Both birds, as befits those harbingers of death that plagued Coleridge's Ancient Mariner, are white as bone. But relative size is difficult to estimate in flying birds at sea, which are far larger than they usually appear from the rolling deck, and other fine points can be just as frustrating. One must know that, among other things, the royal's yellow bill and leading wing edge almost pure white in every plumage distinguish it from the more variable wanderer, which has a pink bill and a checkered wing edge.

One can watch albatrosses for hours, like rough surf or fire. The wandering and the royal are attended all day by two smaller *Diomedea,* the black-browed and the gray-headed albatross. In sweeping crescents, the great birds cross the bow, hurtle aft down past the ship, bank upward and around, crossing the wake. The albatross feeds mainly on slippery squid—hence the hooked design of its great beak—while the petrels and shearwaters glean small organisms from the surface plankton.

Despite marked differences in size and "jizz,"[6] all species in this large oceanic group share a locking mechanism in the wing, which permits the bird to hold a gliding course with little effort. As Victor observes, our human intelligence has yet to design a wing or "plane" impelled by wind that can fly all but motionless for hour after hour, as the gale birds do. Visible from the rail in the larger species are external nostrils in the form of tubal structures on the upper mandible that convey a briny solution from salt glands in front of the eyes. This remarkable evolutionary adaptation permits them to subsist without fresh water. Thus juveniles of the wandering albatross, before their first return to natal breeding grounds, may wander the oceans for four or five years without setting webbed foot on land.

Captain Nikolai Apekhtin is a tall, stalwart, thoughtful man who, I suspect, prefers his classical music to making small talk with his passengers. Captain Apekhtin and his cheerful officers have kindly opened the wide and roomy bridge, which has outdoor extensions to port and starboard; the hardier passengers man the bows, stern, and bridge roof, moving from one vantage point to another in pursuit of passing birds. Today six petrel species are recorded, including the Kerguélen petrel, which like the royal albatross, has ridden the strong westerlies around the bottom of the world from its cold, windy breeding islands in the Indo-Pacific quadrant of the Southern Ocean. Across the distance sail dark sooty shearwaters, long-winged and more elegant than their compact petrel cousins; birds of temperate seas, the shearwaters will disappear after today.

Wearing the scarlet anoraks or parkas supplied them by the tour company, bracing binoculars with elbows on the rails, our passengers form a red wedge in the bows. Ducking cold spray, they scan the waves, swap field marks, and drop bird names. Most are cheerful veterans of past field trips[7] who have saved up for this Antarctic voyage for the joy of observing oceanic wildlife, which can be challenging and yet fulfilling as one's eye sharpens with increased experience and a deeper knowledge of natural history. It can also be amicably competitive, since even the field leaders, and especially occasional leaders such as I, make mistakes of identification that their colleagues will gleefully call to their attention.

The expedition high point for most birders is the "lifer"—a species clearly seen for the first time and duly added to one's lifetime list. The life lists of experienced field birders are careful and hard-won (if less than impeccable, they have no point) serving mainly as records of the wonderful wild creatures observed and as happy reminders of the places and good company—or bad, as the case may be—they were observed in. Such lists are probably as dependable as those kept by the so-called listers, those avid but not necessarily more expert birders who primarily concern themselves with numbers of recorded species rather than the wonder of the bird itself.

AT 5 P.M. YESTERDAY, the *Ioffe*'s location was 200 nautical miles[8] due south of the Falkland Islands. During the evening, the winds abated and the ocean calmed—six-foot waves rather than twelve, with whitecaps replacing the broad wash made by cresting seas—and at daybreak, the seabirds are still plentiful. Though none but the giant petrel dog the ship, others course the blue roil of the wake for planktonic bits stirred to the surface by the propellers or carve wide circles around the ship before sailing on across the waves toward fathomless horizons.

Small diving-petrels buzz over the waves, and the small slate blue petrels known as whalebirds or prions dart and twist, and black storm-petrels, so diminutive and fragile in the ocean wastes that one wonders what becomes of them in ocean storm, dance at the crests, feet pattering, they flutter down into the troughs. Most are the widespread Wilson's storm-petrel, known to old-time mariners (who perhaps ate it) as "Mother Carey's chicken." Like the sooty shearwaters, this small, black, white-rumped species is a bird of home, abundant in the northern summer off my own North Atlantic coast on the east end of Long Island.

As hours pass, the birds' arcs rise and fall in the long rhythms of the rising, falling bow, their numbers and their species ever changing. In our turning world, within the circle of horizons, *Homo sapiens* is the only species whose numbers will be constant day by day, barring a fall overboard or some fatal misadventure. Like the gale birds, we birders follow our own rhythms in the daily round of feeding and sleeping, moving from cabin and dining salon to bridge and bow, on the lookout even as we circumambulate the lower deck and climb the ladders, leaning into the ship's roll, and round again, around again, world without end, Amen.

POLAR FRONT

The ship's course is transecting the Polar Front or Antarctic Convergence where the South Atlantic meets the northern regions of the Antarctic Ocean. Here polar water, heavy and more dense, sinks hundreds of feet below the surface of the warmer ocean before continuing a northward "creep" that is detectable by hydrologists all the way to the Equator and beyond. In these latitudes, the Polar Front, pushed far southward in the region of Cape Horn by the strong easterly currents of the Cape Horn Drift, is bending north again between the Falklands and South Georgia, sometimes as far as 52° south latitude.

In the so-called sub-Antarctic zone, the Falklands lie north of the Polar Front while South Georgia is well south of it. In winter, the line of the Front marks the northern limit of the Antarctic pack ice, which at this time of year—the austral summer—is in gradual retreat toward the Pole. Even so, I notice a sharp drop in temperature in the sea wind out on deck, for the water is suddenly 5° colder. The Front is a distinct faunal boundary between zones of different temperature, salinity, and nutrient concentrations, inhabited by differing communities of plants and animals, and many bird species observed north of the Front have already vanished, not to be seen again until the *Ioffe* returns north across the boundary on her way from Antarctica toward Cape Horn.

The Polar Front, encircling Antarctica, follows the south boundary of a huge ocean river contained not by continental coasts but by other great bodies of water. The Earth's three main oceans, separated by the continents, are all merged in the far south by this circumpolar current, whose strong easterly set, impelled in turn by the Earth's rotation and the wind, was first noted by master mariner James Cook in the course of his southerly explorations.

Whereas Arctic climates are moderated by warm currents from the south, Antarctica is cut off entirely by its circumpolar river, which never leaves these icebound latitudes and draws minimal heat from the sun. It is, in effect, this girdle of near-freezing water that maintains the polar ice cap and affects climates all around the world. The masses of frigid air moving seaward from the ice collide with the more temperate air over the ocean, creating a broad belt of heavy fog, wild storm, and swirling blizzard, with immense high seas, all of which served as formidable barriers to Captain Cook and all subsequent seekers of the Anti-Arctic or Antarctic— the Terra Australis Incognita, the Unknown Southern Land that Aristotle and Pythagoras and all early geographers supposed must lie at the bottom of the globe, if only to keep the Earth in balance on its axis.

In a map of 1570, the Terra Incognita was thought to fill an immense emptiness south of 50° south latitude—a prescient instinct, since this latitude is the approximate northerly extent of an ice pack, which exceeds all of South America in area.

TOWARD DUSK, the first iceberg, ghostly in the mists, looms off the starboard bow eight or nine miles away. By radar measurement, the ice mountain is several miles in length. Broken off or calved from the seaward face of the great Antarctic ice shelves, these flat-topped sheer-sided monoliths, up to 300 feet high, are only the tip of icebergs whose invisible mass may extend more than a thousand feet below the surface. The largest bergs may endure long enough to wander north beyond the Polar Front, as far as 35° south latitude, before disintegrating entirely.

In 1992, an iceberg 62 by 30 miles in extent, known as 10A, broke off the Ross Ice Shelf and moved north, leaving the Ross Sea to drift eastward on the circumpolar current. Arriving this year in the shipping lanes of the Drake Passage, it is moving at present in the general direction of South Georgia.

In dim gray light and fleeting rays of sun, the toiling seas turn molten, and still the great birds glide through the endless twilight, carving the cold air on rigid wings. The larger petrels, rising and falling in swifter arcs, stitch the horizon line, while the smaller vanish behind frosting crests and scud through long, deep caverns of the troughs. When dark descends, the starless night seems blacker than the night before, and the seas diminish to a strange near calm, as if the ship had entered empty regions beyond all known boundaries, those voids marked "Here Be Dragons" on the ancient charts.

At daybreak the air is already much colder. A majestic iceberg in the south is tinted pale gray-blue, the same gray-blue as the small whalebirds that spin through the dim sunshine, in erratic flight under the bows and over the blue wake. Though the wandering albatrosses and giant-petrels are still with us, the royal albatrosses have vanished, and petrels of more temperate seas have been replaced by such cold-water species as the blue petrel and the Antarctic prion. Soon small penguins turn up in the waves—chinstrap penguins that have swum hundreds of miles from their nearest floe or rock ledge at South Georgia. A seal head surfaces to watch the passing ship; no whales are seen. Black sea and gray cold. The blowing crests throw half-frozen sheets of foam that no longer dissolve, but linger long enough to sheet the downwind face. Late tomorrow afternoon, South Georgia's white massifs will rise from the horizon.

Toward midnight on January 23, the *Ioffe* passes north of South Georgia's northeast cape, off the rock islet called Bird Island. Here she slows, not wishing to draw too near the coast in darkness. In thin blowing snow, in the strong beam of her spotlight, Antarctic prions flutter like pale bats. Confused by the glare, a diving-petrel, then a gray-headed albatross, alight on the upper deck; they cannot get traction to fly off the hard surface or flee capture, and so we hold them, awed by the hollow-boned lightness of these birds and the fright that shines the black bead of the eye. Released with a gentle upward toss, each vanishes instantly out of the light into snow blackness.

The common diving-petrel, which we observed in the troughs of ocean waves south of the Falklands, occurs all around the Southern Ocean from Cape Horn to Macquarie Island, south of Tasmania. Though both species occur in South Georgia waters and are very similar, the black-eyed silent little bird that we cup in our hands tonight is the Georgian diving-petrel, which having adapted to colder temperatures and different plankton species in its diet, breeds south of the Polar Front.

Diving-petrels, black above and white below, are small, short-winged, stubby birds whose buzzing flight is quite unlike that of their long-winged kin. In a striking example of parallel evolution (their avian lineages, developed thousands of miles apart, are only very distantly related), they closely resemble the auks or alcids of the northern oceans such as the dovekie, murre, and puffin. The diving-petrels, it is thought, may actually be evolving toward the flightless condition of the penguins.

SOUTH GEORGIA

Remote South Georgia, 870 miles from the nearest landfall at the Falklands, is listed among the cold, grim, windy, rain-swept, and remote islands close to the Polar Front—the so-called "sub-Antarctic islands"—but in fact, being glaciated and entirely treeless, it is more like an outpost of Antarctica. (The snow line on South Georgia, as Dr. Murphy once observed,[9] is lower than the tree line on Tierra del Fuego, though both lie close to 54° south latitude.)

South Georgia was first sighted in 1675 by a London merchantman blown far off course in an attempt to round the Horn; it was not reported a second time until nearly a century later, by the Spanish ship *Leon* (1756). Captain James Cook, arriving aboard H.M.S. *Resolution* two decades later, gave no credence to the first report and very little to the second, though eventually he deigned to credit the *Leon*'s captain with having inspired its true discovery by an Englishman—in short, himself.

On his first voyage in 1768, Captain Cook's official destination had been Tahiti, which was deemed the most auspicious place from which to observe the transit of Venus across the sun, but his unofficial mission was to locate and claim for England the elusive Terra Incognita whose existence had been rumored for 2,000 years. On his voyage around the South Pacific, Cook charted various locations, including the east coast of Australia, but failed to locate a large landmass farther south. On a second voyage (1772 to 1776), still intent on the lost continent, he probed the ice and crossed the Antarctic Circle three times, reaching 71° 10 minutes south latitude before retreating northward and proceeding east around the Horn, stopping at South Georgia and the South Sandwich Islands before his return to England.

At Possession Bay, on South Georgia's leeward coast, on a summer day of January 1775, having landed officially at three locations, "we displayed our Colours and took possession of the Country in His Majesty's name under a discharge of small arms fire." Though he named it for his sovereign, "mad" George III, Cook had no liking for this ocean rampart of glacier and black rock, with its bludgeoning winds and grim gray weather, and departed at once. He had come in search of this "savage and terrible" place in the hope that it might turn out to be a northern cape of the white continent, which, to judge from South Georgia, he noted in disgruntlement, "would not be worth the discovery." However, his ship would bring to England the exciting news of the great companies of seals and whales in the island's waters, which led to intensive exploration of Antarctic waters.

The slaughter of fur seals was well under way by 1790, and in 1800, 122,000 of these animals were skinned out at South Georgia in a single year. The following year, an American sealer, Captain Edmund Fanning of New York, harvested 57,000 furs, in what is thought to be the most profitable sealing voyage ever made. (A Fanning descendant, perhaps come to pay respects at the fountainhead of the family fortune, is among our passengers.) Within two decades, British sealer James Weddell would report that South Georgia's fur seals "are now almost extinct." Confined to outlying rocks such as Bird Island, they vanished for more than a hundred years before repopulating the main island and regaining their present numbers. Meanwhile, the crews had turned their clubs on the huge elephant seals, whose hides had no market but whose blubber could be boiled down for its oil. The abounding penguins, fatally tame, were used to fuel those fires; later they were boiled down on their own account. In the Falklands in 1867, a single ship harvested 50,000 gallons of penguin oil, the end product of a half million birds; near the Cape of Good Hope 30 years later, some 700,000 African (jackass) penguins were taken, together with their eggs.

The rorqual whales abundant in these waters—the blue whales, fin whales, and their kin—proved too swift for the sailing ships, which had depended on the great slow baleen species of the northern oceans. While the northern right whale and its close relative the bowhead supported the Greenland whaling industry for centuries, the southern right whales were apparently too scattered to support an industry. However, the 19th-century invention of the explosive harpoon gun, fired from the bows of steam-powered ships, permitted the exploitation at South Georgia and throughout the Southern Ocean of the cachalot or sperm whale (for its spermaceti oil) and the rorquals (for their baleen), including the humpbacks and the huge finbacks and blue whales.

OVER THE NIGHT, for want of a good anchorage, the *Ioffe* remains offshore, easing southeast along the coast at half speed. By daybreak, she is off Possession Bay. On a brilliant morning, in the first full sunshine of the voyage, the snow peaks and glaciers glisten under an ice blue sky—we are lucky indeed, for by all accounts, such a day is rare in the sub-Antarctic weather of South Georgia, where even in this summer season, the verdant greens of its grassy hillsides, headlands, and shore benches are normally swept gray by fog and rain.

At the mouth of great Cumberland Bay, black cliffs fall steeply to the water, and below the cliffs, on rocky beaches, the white breasts of king penguins shine amid black boulders. Nearer, the sun catches the large gold ellipses behind each eye on the heads of swimming penguins of this striking species, and also the bright yellow-gold head tufts of the much smaller macaroni penguins and the round heads of fur seals, like dark shining stones. Antarctic prions twist past the ship in scattered companies, like blown confetti, while overhead fly kelp gulls and Antarctic terns—the first coastal birds seen since leaving South America.

Dead ahead, down the eight-mile length of the blue bay, crystal ice walls form the rampart of the broad glacier, descending through thin and shifting mists from Mount Nordenskjöld, 7,725 feet above the sea. (The island's highest peak, Mount Paget, thrusts almost two miles into the sky.) The glaciers between towers of black rock are the dominant element in a forbidding landscape that humbles the white vessel a half mile offshore.

Astonishingly, the water between ship and shore is jade green from the density of organic matter, for in summer, the sea is "supersaturated" with oxygen, a condition that produces high concentrations of hydrogen and iron, phosphates and nutrient salts, which in turn support the myriad diatoms, which feed the clouds of plankton, which feed the fish, birds, and mammals. In Antarctic waters, the most abundant creature in the plankton is the prawnlike *Euphausia superba*, known as krill. Originally a collective term for whale food used by Norwegian whalers,[10] krill may be found, as Dr. Murphy says,[11] "in practically all stomachs of penguins, petrels, pelagic seals, and whales in the far south." For reasons well explicated by the oceanographer Sir Alister Hardy, who studied plankton here on an expedition of 1925-26 that investigated the region's potential for commercial whaling, South Georgia supports one of the Earth's great concentrations of marine creatures:

> South Georgia is a long narrow island, some 100 miles long by some 15 across placed almost at right angles to the main westerly drift. The currents set up round it will be like those set up round any long object forced sideways through a fluid.... Where the main ocean current from the west strikes the continental shelf of South Georgia, there will be an upwelling of water rich in phosphate from the deeper layers on the west side of the island, and it is here that we get the densest growth of diatoms, which are carried round either end into the area behind the island.... Here in this sheltered water are all the Euphausians, young and old, which feed on the diatoms. This is perhaps why South Georgia, so peculiarly situated, should be one of the richest whale-feeding grounds of the world.

Even in Dr. Murphy's time, when the shore whaling stations and steamship whaling were already well established, the huge cetaceans were still abundant; by the end of the 20th century, the great whales were all but gone. A solitary spout on the gray horizon west of South Georgia was the only one I saw in the open ocean during the thousand-mile voyage from Tierra del Fuego.

AT GRYTVIKEN

In King Edward Cove, under a snow peak, lies the rust-roofed hulk of Grytviken, the first whaling station established in the Antarctic; its founder was the Norwegian whaler-sealer Captain Carl Anton Larsen, who leased the site from Great Britain in 1905. The whalers did not have far to go, since so many spouts could be seen from shore that the harpooners had no need to leave the bay. With a labor force of some 300 men, the factory winched as many as twenty-five 60-foot whales each day onto these platforms, to be flensed and cooked not only for whale oil from the blubber but for bonemeal, meat meal, meat extract, and frozen meat. (After whale oil lamps were replaced by kerosene, then electricity, the oil was used mainly for cooking oils and margarine, but the flexible "whalebone" or baleen was still prized for ladies' corsets.) During the six months of the year when the ice relented, the station was serviced by tanker ships from Norway, bringing fuel, food, and equipment and taking away whale products. Some 174,000 whales are thought to have been slaughtered out of Grytviken alone, including a 110-foot blue whale measured here in 1912—the largest creature ever measured anywhere on Earth, not excluding the immense dinosaur called *Brontosaurus* (now *Apatosaurus*).[12]

At Grytviken, after less than a decade of man's use, "slimy waters lapped loathsome foreshores, polluted by offal and refuse.... Viewed through the reeking atmosphere even the magnificent inland scenery seemed to grow tainted and lose its splendor."[13] So wrote Frank Hurley, the inspired photographer of Ernest Shackleton's Imperial Trans-Antarctic Expedition, which sailed from this harbor in November 1913 for the south coast of the Weddell Sea despite dire warnings from the whalers that his ship might be trapped by ice should she venture so far south too early in the season. The whalers at Grytviken were the last to see *Endurance,* which a year later was given up for lost.

The seven Norwegian whaling stations established on the island persisted erratically for 30 years, until the last of them closed down. As the large whales became more difficult to locate, operations were transferred to factory ships and the whalers made do with smaller species such as the common minke, which the whale-eating Japanese pursue to the present day. For a few years after the Europeans left, during the thirties, a Japanese company moved into the station for purposes of "experimental whaling" (which turns out to have included an illegal slaughter of the recently protected humpback and other species), but finally they, too, abandoned Grytviken. On the walls of the museum is a Japanese chart showing how each part was used, for everything from gut strings for tennis rackets to intestine sushi: The number of whale products had increased as the whales declined. "Nothing is wasted but the whale itself," as I once wrote of a sperm whale rendering factory near Durban, South Africa.[14]

Tim and Pauline Carr, a nomad British couple who came by sailboat, tarried here, and established a small museum in the course of a dilatory round-the-world voyage from England, have spotted just two whales from shore in the past five years. Today is the sixth day of sun in the past three months, according to the Carrs, the first year-round inhabitants since whaling days. Awaiting their departure is their century-old *Curlew,* a pretty 28-foot gaff-rigged wooden cutter unencumbered by motor or radio that lies tied up to the half-sunken hulk of the old whale-catcher *Petrel.* The Carrs, who love the enormous silence of this place, are looking for a livelihood that would permit them to stay. Historically South Georgia has been locked in ice through the long winters, but in the warming climate of recent years, it has been ice free. Though there is no place for an airstrip on such steep terrain, a small community of like-minded souls, they say, might be supplied by sea all year-round from the Falkland Islands.

South Georgia was the first territory reconquered by that old warhorse Margaret Thatcher in the "Falklands War" between Argentina and Great Britain—something less than a bitterly fought campaign since the island at that time was uninhabited. The British government had claimed the Falklands—called the Malvinas by the Argentines—in 1833, before their outlying islands could be formally attached by the young governments in South America, but the claim has always been contested by Argentina, which allied itself to Germany in World War II and continued to challenge British influence and jurisdiction all the way south to the Antarctic Peninsula. In March 1982, an Argentine company with a contract to salvage scrap metal from the old whaling stations hoisted the Argentine flag. On April 3, the day after the Argentines invaded the Malvinas, they also seized the old Strömness whaling station on South Georgia. Six Royal Navy vessels soon turned up to reclaim the island, and on June 14, the Argentine forces in the Malvinas/Falklands would surrender. Subsequently, a British "presence" on South Georgia was established here at Grytviken by a postmaster and a small garrison, and today a company of Gurkha soldiers occupies the barracks on the point just beyond the cold and silent abattoir of whales. There they battle homesickness and boredom, their only foes in this overwhelming landscape.

In a rare official action (the first and perhaps the last such action in its history), the ghostly administration of "the British Dependent Territory of South Georgia and the South Sandwich Islands," housed in some cubby in the Falklands, has sent orders forbidding our young Argentine stewardess Letitia Carazco and her brother Dario, a crewman, to so much as set foot ashore. Shrugging off this bureaucratic nonsense, the two kids banter cheerfully with the homesick soldiers, who had been invited to an outdoor barbecue on the ship's stern.[15]

Since 1965, when the factory closed, the introduced reindeer that wander among the bleak wind-battered buildings of the old factory have been joined by enterprising seals and bold king penguins, which rule the ruins of man's works and days. Huge elephant seals lie in groaning rows by the shed walls, and a lively nursery of fur seal pups rushes about on the grassy slope below the grass-grown cemetery. On South Georgia, the once extirpated pinnipeds have made an astonishing comeback, with more than a million fur seals and some 300,000 elephants, and have expanded their range southward to the Antarctic Peninsula, apparently as a result of the Earth's warming climate.

On a tundra hillside above Grytviken, I slaked my thirst from a small brook threading its way down among the tussocks—the ancient pristine water of the glaciers, still uncontaminated by the airborne chemicals of industry and fossil fuel extraction that, elsewhere in the world as beneficiaries of unfettered enterprise, we are sentenced to absorb with every breath. But even here in an ocean fastness far from man's filthing activities, a person dining on a Grytviken reindeer might be slow-poisoned: The Inupiat of the north Alaskan coasts, who before the coming of Big Oil to Prudhoe Bay lived a thousand miles from the nearest gross pollution, were contaminated long ago by eating caribou, which transmit the wind-borne poisons absorbed by the tundra lichens on which they graze.

FORTUNA BAY

That afternoon, duly registered with the territorial government, the *Ioffe* sails out past Barff Point (a location pointed out with affectionate malice to the few unlucky passengers not yet recovered from the roll of the open sea) and heads northwest along the coast to Fortuna Bay. Carved out over long millennia by the Fortuna Glacier, the east wall of the Bay's amphitheater is steep brown shale, but on the west slope, which descends from an ice field dirtied by blown dust, green moss and tussock grass have taken hold above the beach, which is strewn with seals. In the bay, the ship anchors offshore, and we disembark in a squadron of four Zodiacs—tough inflatable outboard boats of rubberized canvas that ferry small shore parties to the beach. Run by a crewman, each Zodiac carries about 12 passengers, all suitably attired in full rain gear to fend off cold spray.

My ascent to a squalling gentoo colony high on a grassy knoll is protested by sprawled elephant seals, named for the male's notable proboscis as well as his dimensions. In halfhearted attempts to bluff intruders, these jiggling behemoths open small mouths wide with weary sighs and deeply aggrieved yawnings. Others have hauled their vast avoirdupois a hundred yards uphill into the tussock, a stupendous feat for a creature up to 20 feet in length, two tons in weight, which can scarcely elevate its body but must hitch itself over the ground with fore flippers alone. The hind flippers in true seals serve only as rudders, useless when ashore, and the name of their taxonomic order, Pinnipedia (in some texts, suborder)—literally, "winged-footed ones"—better describes them in the sea, where these giants among seals are powerful and graceful, descending more than 3,000 feet in pursuit of squid and fish and undertaking journeys that may extend well over a thousand miles; a South Georgia elephant, fitted out with a transmitter, has been tracked to Peter I Island, off the Antarctic coast, about 1,500 miles away.

The elephants peer through lustrous eyes like strangely glazed black moons, blind looking because no pupil is visible. The empty eyes remind me of the great white shark—could this be a parallel adaptation for deep-sea vision? Though some may rear up their small heads and open their pink mouths, punctuating their direful moans and groans with barks, snarls, coughs, and snuffles, their large canines are used mostly in male warfare; they contest no territory with *Homo sapiens* and are rarely inspired to attack, though a friend of the Batemans who took their lethargy for granted lost a part of his calf in passing one too close.

The gentoo colony on its grassy knoll is set about with small stones brightened by a red-flowering rosaceous herb *(Acaena)* and a bright orange lichen *(Placodium)*. The gentoo has a long brush tail, bright coral bill, and a white band across the crown behind the eye. Endowed with a flat lens for underwater viewing, all penguins are a bit nearsighted on land, and as I climb up to the colony, approaching quietly, a few birds actually run toward me, rocking from side to side as penguins do and holding small flipper wings out wide as if to embrace my knee—Welcome, Excellency! Others, less sociable, crouch down in an attempt to hide—no simple matter for a bird of 16 pounds, which, though not large for a penguin, approaches the dimensions of a Christmas goose. Others take advantage of the intrusion by stealing pebbles from the nest of any unwary neighbor that leans off its eggs to obtain a better look. Occasionally a nester throws its head straight back, bill pointed at the heavens, the better to utter its sad braying call. While not abundant anywhere—their total populations scarcely exceed a million birds—gentoos are circumpolar, occurring all around the Southern Ocean.

In the grass lie the pierced and broken shells of penguin eggs pirated by marauding skuas, those heavy pelagic relatives of gulls whose hooked black beaks ravage the eggs and young of other birds and force the adults to relinquish food on land as well as in the air and far at sea. Awaiting their chance, three skuas stand like brown sentinels on rocks and hummocks, or stalk among the nesting birds with spraddled gait.

Far away up the small streams that descend from the glacier snowfields, a broad white area is transformed by binoculars into a large company of king penguins, an estimated 7,000 pairs. Making my way along the shore through gangs of feisty fur seal pups and strolling companies of kings, I ascend a gravel stream a mile or more to the main flock. The kings wail a little, shift a little, but otherwise take scant notice of man's approach, an indifference that cost them dearly in the bad old days when they were herded to the beach to be used as fuel.

After the great emperor, this kingly bird is the second largest penguin and, by common accord, the most beautiful of all its kind. The small, dense feathers of its dorsal surface are a dark, lustrous gray-blue, set off by a rich fire color on the lower mandible and on elegant curved patches behind the eyes that join in a golden swath under the throat; on the upper breast, the fire fades to sunshine yellow, which gives way in turn to the satin ivory of the belly. Our late friend and colleague, the great artist-ornithologist Roger Tory Peterson, who was also an occasional field leader for Victor's company, chose "King Penguin" as the bird name by which Victor's birding friends are known, at least to Victor. Victor is "Warbler" because the wood warblers of the Americas are his favorite group, and I am "Curlew" because of my book *The Wind Birds*, an account of North America's sandpipers and plovers.

While some of the kings have trekked up onto the snows, most are content to stand in the icy stream. Overheating in the summer weather, the panting penguins stand open-beaked, backs to the wind, lifting flippers, feathers, and even big clawed feet for ventilation. In severe cold, feet and bill are tucked in, and the birds face into the wind to hold the feathers closed, since feathers provide most of their insulation; both kings and emperors may lean back onto heels and tail to minimize contact with the ice.

Most birds in the flock have laid no eggs because they are still feeding last year's chicks; raising two chicks every three years, this species can claim the longest breeding cycle among the penguins. The big brown young chirp in a rich warble quite unlike the eerie metallic wailing of the adults, which know their young by voice and not appearance. The chicks stand about looking disconsolate or trudge along after their parents, bill pointed down, eyes to the gravel, in a manner that says, Well, *this* life is no fun! So fluffy are they, and so thick their down, that they cannot fully lower their flippers, and their short tails are scarcely visible. Many are currently in the molt that precedes juvenile plumage, and even those near completion of this process sport odd tufts of fluff on breast or back; one hopelessly foolish and appealing chick would look like an adult without fire color except for a large cock-eyed tuft on one side of its head but not the other. As yet, the chicks neither dive nor swim well—penguins are only minimally buoyant—and when one ventures into the salt shallows, it may be attacked by skuas and giant-petrels, which harass and peck it until it is exhausted, whereupon it is greedily pulled to pieces.

In addition to gentoos (120,000 pairs, mainly in small colonies in these sheltered glacier bays) and kings (about 200,000 pairs, in about 30 colonies), there are some 2,000 pairs of chin straps and perhaps 2.5 million macaronis on South Georgia; almost all the macaronis nest on inaccessible steep headlands across the island on the windward coasts. Though confined to the Western Hemisphere, the gold-crested macaroni, named for some putative resemblance to certain 19th-century Italian dandies called by that name, is the most abundant of all penguins, with an estimated 12 million pairs.

PRION ISLAND
AND SALISBURY PLAIN

On January 25, just before dawn, the ship sails from Fortuna Bay, bound west for the Bay of Isles, where a madding crowd of 40,000 kings stand about on salt flats known as Salisbury Plain. But on this gray day, a 35-knot wind is blowing from the east, with heavy sea mist, and even inside the Bay of Isles, the beach is exposed to an onshore swell too burly for the Zodiacs, which land instead on the lee shore of Prion Island. Here the boat parts a ghostly flock of several thousand whalebirds, swirling over a bed of giant kelp like a hatch of flies.

On shore, a rude gang of South Georgian fur seals, protective of new pups, does its best to drive its would-be admirers from its turf. The nearby elephants groan dismally at the uncouth uproar made by *Arctocephalus* ("Bear Head") as it threatens *Homo* with bodily assault.

Unlike the elephants, fur seals are not true seals, related to the otters, but eared seals, whose ancestry is closer to the dogs and bears: The best known eared seal is the California sea lion or "circus seal," trained to snatch tossed fish out of the air and balance red balls on its nose. Eared seals have small external ears rather than ear holes and dense underfur with a thin blubber layer instead of the reverse, but the difference of most concern to their would-be admirers is their rapid terrestrial locomotion. Unlike true seals, recumbent when ashore, eared seals can rear up on strong fore flippers that elevate the heavy head and chest, and furthermore can turn their hind flippers forward to function as crude feet, permitting forward motion on four limbs in a kind of rocking canter. Aggressive on their breeding territories and wherever they tend young, they have no difficulty overtaking—nor reluctance about biting—mammal visitors unless deterred by shouts or sticks or dexterous parries with a tripod.

Most of the fur seals lie inland from the beach, concealed in the eroded gullies between high tussocks, from where they frequently rush forth from ambush, roaring and growling, brown teeth bared, in a bluff charge, which, unless discouraged, may turn into a real one. Even the otter-faced pups practice attack, with a sharp, disagreeable yapping. As an intrepid field leader charged with the protection of the visitors, I am armed with a light wand to distract and deflect them, but since we are not authorized to swat these large foul-mouthed assailants, I am mainly reduced to tremulous roarings and bluff charges of my own. Not until all visitors are shepherded through the gantlet to the safety of an uphill path does Bear Head back away into its lairs to brood and grumble.

From Prion's summit perhaps 60 feet above the sea, the green islet of grass and sphagnum moss, in a tundra of bogs, hillocks, and small ponds, rolls away into the mists: a pair of yellow-billed pintail, battling this wind, fly up from a tundra pool.[16] On a conical nest of mud and grasses built up two feet or more to its shallow bowl, a wandering albatross sits unperturbed, its white wings folded neatly around it; the exquisite black vermiculations on the scapular feathers of this monumental bird make one gasp at the meticulousness of its creation. Staring rudely from 20 feet away, I study the "tube nose" apparatus that permits the disposal of the salt extracted from ocean water. In the albatross this tube has twin passages, one on each side of the upper mandible, while in the shearwaters and petrels, the upper mandible is straddled by a single tube.

The albatross, as still as alabaster, never so much as turns its head for a better look at its tormentor, which suggests that as in camouflaged nesters, the instinct of this big white thing assures it that by maintaining perfect stillness it remains unseen. All the way down the island ridge, others sit like white boulders in the tussock, breasting the hard east wind.

The wandering and gray-headed albatrosses, which breed mostly on South Georgia, are among the 17 albatross species currently endangered by longline ocean fishing. Like many seabirds, albatrosses will follow commercial vessels that toss food scraps overboard, including the thousands of baited hooks that are set on longlines in the wake for deepwater species such as swordfish, tuna, and the Antarctic toothfish, or "Chilean sea bass," all of which are endangered, in their turn, by overfishing; seizing the baits before they sink, the birds are dragged under and drowned—a needless slaughter, since a number of devices already developed would forestall the destruction of an estimated 300,000 seabirds every year.

Flitting about among the tussocks is the "lark" noted by Captain Cook, a dark brown passerine with blackish streaking and white outer tail feathers—the South Georgia pipit, the only songbird endemic to the island and the most southerly land bird anywhere on Earth. Since sealing days, escaped ship rats have eliminated this ground-nesting species from the main island, but it has managed to persist on offshore islets. The small pipit and perhaps the ducks are South Georgia's sole native inhabitants in the southern winter: Most gulls, terns, and sheathbills migrate north and west to the Falklands or the continent, while the marine birds and mammals move out to sea. How the pipit subsists through the long, cold, dark months is not known, since no ornithologist has braved the winter to observe it. Presumably it picks organic bits among the ice cakes thrown up by the waves or small crustaceans from the uprooted giant kelp whose bronze tentacles drape the rocky shores.

Here and there sits a rough nest of the brown skua, a bulky cinnamon-colored predator and scavenger that on Prion Island sustains itself mostly on Antarctic prions, to judge from all the blue-gray wings scattered around the prion nesting burrows. On a cliff ledge nest overlooking a deep cove, my binoculars pick out a light-mantled albatross and chick. With its silver mantle and soft warm brown plumage, this albatross is the most elegant of all its family, despite a peculiar addled gaze in which the small black pupil remains on the lower eye rim as if it had got stuck while this cross-eyed bird was contemplating its own egg. In the chick, the pupils are properly centered but the eye appears wildly enlarged by the owlish disk of white down that surrounds it, creating an expression as bizarre as in the adult.

The mist rolling inland from the sea is thickening and the surge increasing, but the weather in the afternoon eases long enough to permit beaching the boats near Salisbury Plain. There a colony variously estimated at from 40,000 to 100,000 king penguins is scattered across the shallow streams and gravel beds and bunchgrass tussocks of the glacial delta. This shore, too, is ruled by *Arctocephalus*, which has many new black pups and the urge to guard them. As before, there are rancorous encounters but no bloodshed.

Within the hour the williwaw known as katabatic wind (from the Greek *katabatikos:* Its lovely translation is "falling wind" or "wind falling from a higher place") descends in a sudden avalanche of dense cold air down off the glacier; its force can flip a Zodiac right over. This day the squall is merely strong, but it comes bearing sleet, then snow. At the ship, heavy four-foot surges slop high up the ship's side, then drop the Zodiacs out from under the gangway platform, imperiling the transfer of the passengers. However, the platform crew is well trained in this task, and birders, even the more elderly, are of necessity more bold and hardy than the ordinary traveler, not easily daunted by discomfort or a drenching, and therefore a pleasure to travel with.

On her return eastward down the coast, the ship edges her way in and out of Strömness Harbor, where three old whaling stations lie decrepit, like abandoned military outposts in the wake of war. Behind the wind-worn barn-red buildings of the Strömness station, a long snow valley climbs to the black peaks and silver glaciers of the island's unexplored interior, which was painfully traversed from the windward coast by the first men who ever crossed the island—men who knew they would surely freeze to death if they ever sank into exhausted sleep or halted long enough to rest before making the perilous descent into this valley. On May 20, 1916, the tough Norse whalers who inhabited these buildings were the first to learn the fate of the *Endurance,* which had sailed from Grytviken for the Antarctic in November 1913, and vanished from the world without a trace.

On January 19, 1914, the ship had been beset by ice deep in the Weddell Sea. For almost a year, she drifted with the ice pack, north and west toward the Antarctic Peninsula, until in November of that year she was crushed by the shifting ice and sunk. For the next five months, her crew dragged two longboats over treacherous ice before they could be launched in open water. Eventually, they arrived at Elephant Island, northwest of the Peninsula, from where, in early April 1916, six men would set out by open boat on an 800-mile voyage over the Southern Ocean toward South Georgia. On April 26, half-dead from exposure after 17 days in the roaring seas, they managed a landing on

South Georgia's dark and desolate windward coast. Shackleton and two companions climbed thousands of feet into the unmapped glaciers of the central range, then trekked southeast for 18 miles across icefalls and ravines before making the perilous descent to the leeward shore here at the Strömness station. "These are men," grunted the astonished Norwegians, who set off at once for the windward coast to rescue the three others. Scarcely recovered, Shackleton sailed as rapidly as possible for Argentina, from where he made two vain attempts to breach the ice and rescue his stranded crew on Elephant Island. A third try on August 30, 1916, was successful; he would famously return his crew to England without the loss of a single man.

Late in December 1921, in chronic ill health and without prospects, Sir Ernest returned with a few of his old crew to this scene of his great survival, as if knowing that his death was near again. At Grytviken, where he died in early January 1922, at age 47, and was buried two months later, we drank champagne at the hero's graveside in the sun and blowing grasses of the whalers' cemetery, to a fanfare of loud groans and blarts from the indifferent elephants.

GOLD HARBOR, DRYGALSKI FJORD, CAPE DISAPPOINTMENT

On this brilliant morning, as swirling snow mist shrouds Mount Paget, the pristine white snow petrel makes its first appearance of the voyage, and the beautiful Cape petrels, called *pintado* for their motley of white-spotted chocolate, and the South Georgia shag, which in various species and geographic races peers with azure eye from wave-washed rocks all around the Southern Ocean.

Three humpback whales that blow and surface off the bow do not move off as the *Ioffe* comes abreast but roll easily along in no great hurry. When at last they sound, their great gleaming flukes, lined white beneath, rise in slow curves like question marks against the white mountains all around, completing their age-old graceful arcs before sliding silently from view beneath the surface.

At noon, the vessel turns inshore past black rock reefs into Gold Harbor. Twin glaciers descend from snow horizons between peaks, in an air as clear as might be found on some frozen planet. Along the edges of the bay, at the foot of steep, bare slopes of scree and grasses, gleam the golden browns of elephants and fur seals, which are scattered the whole length of the mile-long beach and far back into the tussock on the bench behind, their yawp and rumble resonant in the vast amphitheater. In the shallows of the glacier stream where it crosses the gravel beach, 14 elephant bulls recline side by side, as snug as a fresh batch of warm loaves. Each little while, the din and cry of the marine mammals, the tidal whisper on the gravel beach, is shattered by the crack and thunder of the calving glacier, like dynamite in a rock quarry, causing frozen dust to rise where the ice has fallen.

The gravel bars are crowded with king penguins, packed close at the far end of the beach. Inland a mile upstream toward the glacier, at least 50,000 birds are in view at once. Gold auricular ellipses on each bird's sunshined head cast a golden haze over the flock—could this be the provenance of the name Gold Harbor? Pairs of light-mantled albatrosses soar overhead along the cliff rims, and squads of gentoos bustle everywhere like banquet waiters. Wings wide, some come tumbling to greet us as the boats touch shore.

In the shallows, oblivious of man and bathing penguins, young fur seals skirmish in loud splashing flurries. The fur seal congregation is ruled by a group of bull-necked adult males or beachmasters, roaring and false-charging. Brandishing my thin wand, I yelp and jump like some sort of hobgoblin, arms outspread to enlarge my dimensions, as early hominids may have done in attempts to baffle the larger, faster, and far better armed animals on the African savanna. The atavistic screech-and-jump usually halts the charge a few yards away, but one must be alert for a sneak attack after the group has passed. One perceives the canid ancestor in these creatures—a dog of, say, 300 pounds or better.

The fur seals, which sometimes prey on penguins, taking an estimated 10,000 every year here at South Georgia, are in firm command for a considerable distance up the steep side of the headland, which we climb in search of the scattered ledge nests of the light-mantled albatross. Eventually two are located and duly photographed in a dramatic light. One must admire the dedication and endurance of both Batemans, who lug heavy cameras with spare lenses and tripods up steep slopes and will not permit anyone to help them, partly to stay in shape for future lugging and partly because precious equipment might be broken, compounding the loss with an awkward situation. Bob and Birgit are dedicated naturalists and conservationists of generous intelligence and good humor. Though we met once briefly at a snow leopard conference in Seattle, this voyage is an opportunity for real acquaintance, which we consolidate with evening whiskeys in our cabins.

David Reesor of Tucson, a Bateman friend, professes a lifelong disinterest in the class Aves, yet he, too, climbs high to obtain better angles on the cliff face and is rewarded with a fine photographic portrait of this sublime albatross, a copy of which now ornaments my office wall. His recalcitrance reminds me of another friend who has accompanied us on Victor's expeditions to Namibia and Botswana, India and Bhutan, and who much prefers a well-stocked bar to any source of inspiration out-of-doors. Eschewing the burden of binoculars, this man vows that inspecting any bird less than 50 pounds in weight and more than 50 feet away is against his principles, for which reason he is known as "Fifty-Fifty." Unfortunately old Fifty-Fifty isn't here to admire the king penguin, which is apt to approach its admirer rather than flee. In fact, few birds on Earth can rival the king penguin on the 50-50 standard for satisfactory birding in the field.

The photographers work also with the snowy sheathbill, *Chiona alba* (literally "snow white"), at its sensible nest site under an overhang on the cliff face. In size and aspect, and even in its flight, the sheath-bill resembles a heavy white domestic pigeon, but at close hand one sees the unfeathered pink face characteristic of such carrion-feeders as vultures and certain storks, which go about bare-faced to avoid soiling their feathers. *Chiona* makes its living as a nest-robber and scavenger, preying upon eggs and chicks of penguins and other birds, and subsisting in the leaner seasons on old seal placentas, beached carcasses of seals and whales, and other nutritious fare.

Down the beach, sheathbills await the first wrong moves of the king penguins, which construct their nest scrapes on the gravel benches. Thousands of nests are so close together that an occupant may be tempted to lean out and administer a smart peck to its neighbor; in this way, the single precious egg is partly exposed. I arrive just in time to see a skulking sheathbill dart beneath a leaning bird to spike its egg—a serious loss, for what has been stolen is no mere egg, but the entire reproductive essence, the distilled life energy, of the long penguin year at sea. Gold Harbor leaves us excited and astonished by the urgency of life and ever present death in this great amphitheater of silver glaciers on a blue wind-chopped glacier bay that empties out into the polar ocean.

Before departing South Georgia for Antarctica, the white ship enters the Drygalski Fjord, a beautiful passage less than a mile wide, which narrows as it penetrates eight miles into the island's mountain heart to the great glacier under Mount Macklin (6,233 feet).[17] Like the Beagle Channel, Drygalski Fjord is an ancient valley shaped into a U by glaciers moving between mountains. There are few birds in this still channel where the black surface between mirrored walls of white lies sheltered from the wind. A few miles inland, in the inner fjord, snow petrels come and go like lost bird spirits, searching high white walls.

It is already late when the ship emerges from the fjord. Offshore, wandering albatrosses, a few, carve the twilight sky. From the bridge, one can see the island's southeast promontory—black headlands, sea cliffs, and white surf, exploding in the dusk. Captain James Cook, rounding this cape only to be confronted by a rugged coast leading back toward the northwest, and realizing that the mountains of South Georgia were not a coast range of Antarctica, as he had hoped, named the place Cape Disappointment and departed without bothering to map it. This windward coast (where Shackleton would struggle ashore) would remain unmapped until 1819, when a Russian circumpolar expedition under Baron Thaddeus von Bellingshausen did its best to fill in the few omissions on Cook's masterly charts.

At 54°, 42 minutes south latitude, a third of the distance across the South Atlantic toward Africa's Cape of Good Hope, South Georgia is one of the world's most remote points of land; were this ship to proceed due east from Cape Disappointment, she might circle the planet like an albatross, passing well south of Africa, Tasmania, and New Zealand and making her first continental landfall near Cape Horn. Instead she rounds the rock islets off the cape and heads westward and upwind into Stygian blackness and fast-moving squalls; the bow rises and falls on the long swells of the Scotia Sea as she takes her southwest bearing for Antarctica.

SCOTIA SEA

Our course has roughly traced a great submarine mountain system known to geologists as the Scotia Arc, which connects the southern Andes in Tierra del Fuego and Staten Land with the point where high mountains rise again on the arc's farthest outcrop at South Georgia.

One hundred sixty million years ago, when the primordial southern supercontinent known as Gondwana[18] had already started its long fragmentation, its central region, now Antarctica, was still attached to South America, Africa, the Indian subcontinent, and

Australia. A folding and breaking of the plates or shields of the Earth's crust, accompanied by cataclysmic volcanic activity, commenced Gondwana's rifting and disintegration, as long eons of continental drift separated the primordial landmass into the present continents of the Southern Hemisphere, and what is now the Indian subcontinent, breaking away from Africa, pushed slowly into Asia, forcing the Earth's crust five miles into the sky in the great upthrust known as the Himalaya.

In the all but unimaginable epochs required to move whole continents by the inch into a new configuration of the planet's surface, Africa separated from South America along fault lines so precise that the two continents might fit together even today. (Their rocks show that the Falklands were outposts of Africa left stranded on South America's continental shelf.) South America was still attached to a northern extension of Gondwana known today as the Antarctic Peninsula, as demonstrated in the similar rock structure of the Peninsula and the southern Andes. This last connection was finally disrupted some 40 million years ago by the collision of Pacific and Atlantic plates that would skew Tierra del Fuego and Staten Land toward the east. The later separation of New Zealand, then Australasia, as Gondwana disappeared into the icy mists, permitted the formation of a circumpolar river four times the volume of the Gulf Stream. Circling eastward, filling the great rupture between the Peninsula and Cape Horn, this huge current known as the West Wind Drift, encircled and further isolated what remained of Gondwana. By the time this landmass moved over the South Pole in late Ordovician to Devonian times, all that was left of the fragmented land bridge was the mountainous archipelago at the north end of the Antarctic Peninsula where the ship is headed.

Beneath the hull, the Scotia Arc, 2,700 miles long, is rounding in its sickle curve toward the peninsula; these waters within the arc are called the Scotia Sea. In this region long ago, a new tectonic plate collided with the adjacent plate to eastward, causing the uplifting of the

Earth's crust at South Georgia, and also the eruption of lava along a line of volcanic ridges to the southeast whose emergent summits were named "Sandwich Land" by Captain Cook once he had realized that this archipelago, like South Georgia, was unconnected to the missing continent.[19]

Our bearing lies well northwest of the South Sandwich chain, which is chronically locked away by ice and all but unvisited. "The edge of this immense icefield was composed of loose or broken ice so close-packed together that nothing could enter it."Cook wrote in *Toward the South Pole and Around the World,* published in 1777. "It was indeed my opinion as well as that of most on board that this ice extended quite to the pole or perhaps joined some land to which it had been fixed from creation." The South Sandwich Islands were the final landfall on Cook's second circumpolar voyage, which took more than three years, and it was here that the great mariner concluded, "I firmly believe there is a tract of land near the Pole which is the source of most of the ice which is spread over this vast Southern Ocean" (February 6, 1775). Cook was the first to use that term, having recognized the uniformity of climate, winds and currents, and even the marine birds and mammals of this vast sea far to the south of the known world.[20]

The chin strap penguins we see porpoising in mid-ocean have probably come from the South Sandwich coasts, where they are common. (The thin black band around the throat seems to hold its black helmet on the chin strap's head among the white-capped waves.) The birds are more than 500 miles from shore, in strong ocean currents that carry them far from their home rookeries; presumably these are juveniles, which, like the gale birds, may spend two years at sea before returning.

The blithe wandering of penguins in the ocean wastes is made possible by the salt gland adaptation shared with the gale birds and also by the uncanny powers of navigation found in migratory birds, sea turtles, and other endowed creatures, from dogs to spiny lobsters. Perhaps it was also an attribute of early man, but man does not recognize such gifts as true intelligence, being insufficiently intelligent himself to imagine intelligences of a nature different than his own.

Watching for hours from bow and bridge, I am awed by these creatures and their adaptations and migrations, as I also am—please forgive my digressions—by icebergs, whales, the sea and ships, circumpolar currents, geologic time, the origins and evolutionary histories of life-forms, the quirks of birds, birders, and explorers, antifreeze in fish blood, the blue in ice, human folly, the ozone hole, and the earthly balances upset by global warming—in short, the mysteries of the natural world in their endless variations, the myriad petals of creation that open up and fall away in every moment.

Therefore I seek to understand phenomena that might help our self-destroying species to appreciate the shimmering web of biodiversity in the Earth process, the common miracles, fleeting as ocean birds, which present themselves endlessly to all our senses, to be tasted, experienced, and fiercely defended for our innocent inheritors against the rape and dreadful wasting of this beautiful and fragile biosphere and its resources. In the forgetting that we, too, are animals, a part of nature, as dependent on its health and balance as any other mammal, we foolishly permit the unrestrained industrial erosion and poisoning of our Earth habitat that promises to leave mankind as desolate and bereft of hope as a turtle stripped live from its shell.

THIS SOUTHWESTERLY VOYAGE, quartering the prevailing wind of the Furious Fifties, is usually a rough one, and all are relieved that the seas are moderate. In mid-voyage, a solitary sheathbill circles the ship as if considering alighting, then keeps on going, flying strongly in the direction of South Georgia—an odd sighting so far out across the open sea, since its feet are scarcely webbed.

This afternoon, a sudden puff of mist, like an enigmatic sign on the horizon, is disturbing in its loneliness. From the look of its high vertical spout, it is a finback or conceivably a blue whale. Wind and sea continue moderate, with increasing fog. A sky of unbroken pewter gray looks swollen with somber ocean light, on this third day at sea without a sign of ship or aircraft, flotsam or driftwood—no sign that the human mammal has appeared on Earth—only the empty wind and waves, the silent birds passing through monotones sea and sky without a trace. Toward noon, another iceberg looms, sheer-sided and table-topped as a white mesa. In the slate sea, whitecaps torn away by wind seethe across the faces of the waves, and each lacy fan, in its swift instants of life, reveals the same pale aqua blue that is seen in the sea wash along the hull and in the blue-silver churning in the wake. In the rough seas, for all that tumult, all that motion, it is only movement that falls away toward the horizon. Each drop of water, left behind, subsides in place. One is borne away in the ever changing yet eternal ocean rushing past the porthole, as all notions about life dissolve and vanish.

Bird numbers diminish as icebergs increase; not all seabirds are adapted to such harsh conditions. The drifting mountains are composed of polar snows compressed into ice, and the large plateau-topped or tabular bergs, up to 300 feet high, are sections broken off the ice shelves on the continental rim—most likely the Larsen Ice Shelf on the east side of the Antarctic Peninsula, though some may have calved from the Ross Ice Shelf, halfway around the circumference of the continent in the Australian quadrant. Though their surface is white, the ice deep within is a cold transparent blue, as in the glaciers. Blue ice appears when the air spaces are compressed, no bubbles are left, and the ice absorbs light at the red end of the spectrum, permitting its blues to radiate. A blue light may identify a berg freshly broken off the ice shelf, but more often, scoured by salt wind and crusted white with snow and surface freezing, the drifting mass has been weakened and eroded by storm seas and currents, become unstable, and suddenly rolled over, exposing the beautiful blue light within.

Today, the towering ice platforms are never out of sight, with as many as five or six in view at once. Some may have drifted for decades, circling the frozen continent in clockwise orbit. A description by the 19th-century American naval officer Charles Wilkes is the finest I have come across:

> Some of the bergs were of magnificent dimensions … from one hundred and fifty to two hundred feet in height, with sides perfectly smooth, as if they had been chiselled. Others exhibited lofty arches of many-coloured tints, leading into deep caverns, open to the swell of the sea, which rushing in, produced loud and distant thunderings. The flight of birds [snow petrels?] passing in and out of these caverns recalled the recollection of ruined abbeys, castles, and caves, while here and there a bold projecting bluff, crowned with pinnacles and turrets, resembled some Gothic keep.… These tabular bergs are like masses of beautiful alabaster: a verbal description of them can do little to convey the reality to the imagination of one who has not been among them. If an immense city of ruined alabaster palaces can be imagined, of every variety and shape and tint, and composed of huge piles of buildings grouped together, with long lanes or streets winding irregularly among them, some faint idea may be formed of the grandeur and beauty of the spectacle.[21]

Most large bergs, eroding and melting above and below the surface, will vanish within about four years. The bubbles of pure ancient air released during disintegration come from the Earth's atmosphere of long ago, in the perennial snow of the continent's ice mantle. Spending many centuries in the ice sheet as it makes its glacial creep toward the sea, that crystalline air cannot be less than 10,000 years old—the last clean air for the same reason that the iceberg's melt may be the last uncontaminated water on the planet's surface.

Freshwater melt from icebergs in this season encourages the growth of phytoplankton, which nourishes the zooplankton, which supports the clouds of breeding krill on which ocean birds and mammals depend. The krill concentrations that draw baleen whales south into these waters after their breeding seasons are often vast here on the Scotia Arc between South Georgia and the peninsula, an ocean reach that also attracts high numbers of wintering penguins.

In the course of his Antarctic voyages of 1820 and 1821, von Bellingshausen noted an almost daily multitude of whales. Similarly, in 1823, the British sealer James Weddell recorded "great numbers of finned and hump-backed whales" in these Scotia waters (by "finned whale," Weddell may have meant all native rorquals or pleat-throated whales other than the humpback—the blue whale, fin whale, sei, minke, all of which show small dorsal fins when on the surface), but another 50 years would pass before the advent of steam power permitted profitable pursuit of the swifter rorqual species.

Antarctic whaling, once begun, proceeded as swiftly and fatally as at South Georgia. By 1925-26, when factory ships came into use, a fleet of 23 vessels took 7,825 whales in the Antarctic, including 1,855 blue whales and 5,709 finback; in the 1930-31 season it was 31,000, and by the start of World War II the annual kill had increased to about 40,000. In the half century after 1922, when 3,689 blue whales were destroyed, this "sulfur-bottom whale" of the old accounts—the sulfur color is the phytoplankton attached to its ventral surface—would be reduced to its present endangered status: The remaining animals, scattered in world oceans, may be less than a thousand.

Even after the International Whaling Commission imposed limits on the slaughter, meaningful enforcement on these vast reaches of ocean was impossible, and the limits were flouted regularly by Japan and Norway as well as the Soviet Union. Whales everywhere were becoming so reduced that in 1986, all commercial whaling was prohibited in a general moratorium. Despite the ban, Japan still harvests thousands of lesser rorquals or minke whales, ostensibly for "scientific research," although no useful data are produced and the meat is marketed just as before. From what we are learning of business ethics the world over, who can doubt that in harvesting minkes beyond remote horizons, the larger, more endangered whales are taken, too, wherever an outlaw ship can get away with it? At supper in London a few years ago, the dedicated whale biologist Roger Payne, still angry, told me how Russian scientists, after the implosion of the Soviet Union in 1989, had notified their colleagues in other countries that Soviet vessels had regularly slaughtered the proscribed species, including the vanishing blue whale.

The extraordinary Antarctic whale herds reported by all early captains are now gone, and the knowledge of their wasteful destruction leaves a hollow feeling in the heart and gut. No matter what measures we may take, the peaceful leviathans will never recover their numbers because other conditions, not all of them well understood, are intervening to alter their environment. One of these factors, almost certainly, is the decline of the vast swarms of krill attributed to man's activities and creations, notably "the ozone hole" and "global warming."

Krill availability depends on mineral upwellings and the rich nutrition produced not only by icebergs but also by melting pack ice, which during the Antarctic spring, releases clouds of frozen diatoms, algae, and other microscopic life that thrive in the abundant oxygen and sunlight and feed krill larvae, which would perish without it. In the warming winters of the past half century, however, the northern limit of the pack ice has been steadily withdrawing; in recent decades, the ice plains expanded north of the peninsula only one winter out of three. Whatever the causes, krill populations have diminished by an alarming 80 percent since the last full survey in 1981, despite the absence of whale predation, and the last good breeding year in 1995 was not enough to reverse the decline. Should *Euphausia* fail drastically or disappear, many other forms will perish with it.[22]

In recent years, commercial krill fishing has become a factor, though the annual haul of 100,000 tons, mostly by Japan and Russia, seems scarcely critical in a population whose tonnage has been estimated at 3 billion.[23] Yet there is no limit on commercial harvest of the krill, whose swarms are regional in distribution, so that harvesting these concentrations within 50 miles of wildlife colonies can have a strong local effect. At Livingston Island in the South Shetlands, which we shall visit, a monitored study indicates that the fishery has led to a serious mortality among juvenile chin straps, which are not yet experienced in the open-ocean foraging of their parents and cannot subsist on what little food is left closer to shore.

ANTARCTIC APPROACHES

The ship has crossed the 60th parallel of south latitude into the "official" Antarctica referred to in the international treaties signed in 1959. Originally, its territorial integrity was threatened by incipient disputes over the rights to its rich store of minerals, but in the 1980s, the entire region south of the 60th parallel was set aside as an international zone where no nation could claim resource rights, far less exploit them. In 1991, the so-called Madrid Protocol, signed by 43 nations, established full protection of the Antarctic environment as well as "its associated and dependent ecosystems," including restraints on dumping offal and longline fishing for the large Antarctic toothfish. However, there has been "pirate fishing," even by signatories to the treaties.

Our course skirts the northern reaches of the Weddell Sea, named for British sealer James Weddell, who made three Antarctic voyages in the 1820s. On February 22, 1823, he penetrated the drifting pack ice, breaking free into an unknown open sea. Proceeding southward (to a point off Coats Land, not far from where *Endurance* was beset nearly a century later), he reached 74° 15 minutes south latitude—the "furthest south" since Cook. To the south of our course, some 300 miles east of the peninsula, lie the South Orkneys, named by Weddell for the British Orkneys, which lie at the same latitude in the North Atlantic. The archipelago is 90 percent glaciated and, like South Sandwich, is often locked away in heavy pack ice.[24]

The air is colder and the barometer has fallen in the last few hours. Captain Nikolai Apekhtin, on the bridge, expects a storm. But light winds and moderate seas have prevailed throughout the voyage from South Georgia, and the ship arrived off the northern islands of the peninsula around midnight on January 28, having traveled some 720 miles in two days' time.

At two this morning, a few worthy souls rise shivering from their bunks and climb up to the bridge to peer at the first Antarctic landfall. Icebound Clarence Island, a few miles away off the port bow, is clearly visible in the cavernous dusk of midsummer night, a shrouded mass thrust up from the black seas. To starboard rises the sheer rock called Cornwallis Island; beyond Cornwallis, the high, dim silhouette of Elephant Island forms and vanishes in the gray mist to the southwest. That island was named by early sealers for the lugubrious huge pinnipeds on that 12-mile rock that would help sustain the stranded crewmen of the *Endurance* in the long five months between Shackleton's departure in the longboat for South Georgia and their rescue.

One can't help but compare the fearsome odyssey in that longboat with our own voyage. Wet, frozen, and half-starved, those men endured 17 days and 800 miles of a rough ocean crossing in an open boat. That our own warm and well-fed passage in a milder season over that same reach of sea required but 50 hours induces uneasy pangs of inauthenticity.

NORTHERN PENINSULA

The ship proceeds south to the South Shetland Islands, discovered together with its swarming fur seals on February 19, 1819, by Captain William Smith of the brigantine *Williams,* which like many vessels had been blown off course rounding the Horn. Smith's discovery was not accepted by Royal Navy officers stationed at Valparaiso, who sniffed at his claim that he had found outlying islands of the mythical white continent. On October 14 of that year, however, the *Williams* planted the British flag on what is now King George Island, and this time Smith's Valparaiso interlocutor, a Captain Shirreff, took him seriously enough to charter the *Williams* and send her south for the third time under the command of naval officer Captain Edward Bransfield, with Smith as navigator. The voyage confirmed Smith's discovery of the South Shetlands and also the existence of an unknown land some 60 miles to eastward—not another island of white mountains but a northward extension of the continent itself, as confirmed from the air more than a century later, in 1937.

Royal Navy doubts about a mere sealer's discovery were not shared by American and British sealers drawn to the South Shetlands by rumors of Smith's first voyage. First to appear was the ship *Hersilia,* which turned up at Livingston Island on January 21, 1820, a day or two after Bransfield's arrival. At least 30 American and 25 British sealing vessels came that summer, with one ship harvesting 14,000 seal furs in a mere five weeks.

Though Captain Bransfield of the Royal Navy is usually given credit, outer Antarctica's true discoverer appears to have been the unsung William Smith, whose brigantine was sold off for a coal ship once the fur seals were exterminated, and whose plea for recognition and assistance from the British Admiralty in later years would be refused by the same Captain Shirreff who had sniffed at his discovery in 1819, in Valparaiso. Possibly it was also Shirreff who placed Bransfield in command of the *Williams* so that the Royal Navy might be credited with Smith's discovery should it turn out to be valid. Smith died poor and in obscurity 20 years later.[25]

TOWARD 7:30 IN THE MORNING, in the Bransfield Strait, a humpback whale attended by a half-grown calf breeches repeatedly nearby the ship. At 10:15, as the *Ioffe* proceeds southwest to King George Island, another humpback appears off the starboard bow, hurling its mass clear out of the water and descending on its side with an explosion of white, like heavy surf. It erupts again through the slate surface off the beam, close to the ship, and again and then again in the blue-gray wake as it falls astern.

The first Antarctic birds: Across the bow flies the brown-and-white polar petrel called by Captain Cook "the Antarctic peterel." Observing it, Cook reasoned that the unknown land must lie somewhere to the south, for otherwise where would these peterels nest?[26] Toward mid-morning, mist-gray in the gray mist, comes the silver or southern fulmar, noted in Cook's journals as the gray petrel. Both species fly with stiff, quick flaps, then a prolonged glide.

Imagine the fortitude of Captain Cook, tacking upwind under sail in rough seas "pestered" with ice:

> ... the night was exceptionally stormy, thick and hazy, with sleet and snow.... Surrounded on every side with danger, it was natural for us to wish for daylight. This, when it came, served only to increase our apprehensions, by exhibiting to our view, those strange mountains of ice, which in the night we had passed without seeing. —*A Voyage Toward the South Pole and Around the World*

Cook's ambitions in regard to the unknown continent were not always shared by his naturalists and chroniclers, Johann and George Forster, who seemed to question this quixotic, impractical, and exceptionally perilous quest:

> The ice, the fogs, the storms and ruffled surface of the sea formed a disagreeable scene ... the climate was rigorous and the food detestable ... we withered and became indifferent to all that animates the soul. We sacrificed our health, our feelings, our enjoyments to the honour of pursuing a track unattempted before.[27]

In a 20-knot wind, over morose seas of cold, unsettled weather, the ship continues southward, picking her way through passages between icebergs. Unlike those in the Scotia Arc, these great bergs on the Pacific side of the peninsula have probably come from the Ross Ice Shelf and Ross Sea. Some are immense as pinnacled medieval castles, and some are a pale crystalline blue. In sunset light, that clear blue thickens oddly to an opaque plastic.

The outer region of the peninsula, though sheathed in ice, is still well north of the Antarctic Circle and the polar ice cap, and its glaciers are mostly alpine glaciers, filling mountain cirques and overflowing into coastal valleys. From the summits of King George Island, glaciers descend to icy surf and an iron sea touched by cold glimmerings of sun; sea mists drift across towering walls of ice and rock. In this darkening afternoon, hard wind and snow transform the white mountains in the sea into realms of myth.

At Turret Point, the sea surge at the gangways is too high to load passengers into the Zodiacs, much less land them safely on the gravel bench, and so the *Ioffe* continues south to the Polish research station at Arctowski Bay.[28] Here a small pod of humpbacks forages slowly along the black gravel bar, oblivious of the blue whale bones strewn on the beach crest; one great skull appears to be ten feet across.

Down the shore, the bare cheerless yellow shacks, as in many polar stations, serve mainly as a political purchase on Antarctica, supplied by one ship annually.

King George Island has an airstrip that serves the several research stations set up here for the study of, among other things, global warming's role in the recent climate change on the peninsula and the West Antarctic ice sheet. As of this year (1998), 26 nations have established more than one hundred scientific research stations in Antarctica. Although 35 are manned all year around, the meteorological stations that register the weather are mostly untended.

Since 1908, seven nations have staked claims in Antarctica—Argentina, Great Britain, Chile, New Zealand, Australia, France, and Norway—but all claims were waived in 1959 with the ratification of the Antarctic Treaty by the United States and five other nations. Today no nation "owns" Antarctic territory, though there are many pending claims to the valuable minerals in the rock under the ice—gold, silver, platinum, copper, and molybdenum, also some manganese and cobalt. Significant gas and oil deposits have been located under the Ross and Weddell Seas, and huge veins of low-grade coal in the Transantarctic Mountains. The latest amendments to the treaty (1991) ban all mining until 2041—no great sacrifice for the time being, since the technological obstacles and logistical costs of mining a frozen continent encourage the long view.

After a seven-year battle by conservation groups, the treaty's Environmental Protection Protocol has now been ratified by 26 countries; predictably, Japan, Russia, and the U.S. were among the last to sign. In a rare instance of international accord, all visiting aircraft and vessels are monitored to ensure that all waste materials, including empty fuel drums, are removed. Any activity relating to mineral resources other than scientific research is prohibited, as is the introduction of exotic species, dogs included. Strict restrictions on disturbance of wildlife habitat keep visitors at a respectful distance from all wildlife, from nesting birds to seals.

For the moment, Antarctica has no economic activity other than brief seasons of marginal tourism and commercial fishing, both based elsewhere. How long this policy of restraint can be maintained in light of rampant human populations and shrinking resources is another matter. To judge from the stunted market vision of our governments, the signatories to the treaty may eventually abandon its sane policies and proceed unilaterally with resource exploitation, ensuring the ruin of the last clean place on Earth.

TO PAULET ISLAND

Last night the *Ioffe* departed Admiralty Bay on King George Island, crossing the Bransfield Strait toward the peninsula. This morning, in a 30-knot wind, cold spray ices the decks. At d'Urville Island, the ship enters the Antarctic Sound, a broad passage that parts the northern region of the 600-mile peninsula from its main section on the continent and serves as a channel into the vast frozen gulf of the Weddell Sea. Our destination is Paulet Island, north of the sound off the eastern coast.

A volcanic cone 1.7 miles wide and 1,158 feet high, Paulet Island shelters an Adélie colony of some 100,000 pairs. This was fortunate for the redoubtable Captain Carl A. Larsen, master of the ship *Antarctic* on geologist Otto Nordenskjöld's Swedish South Polar Expedition of 1903-1904 and later the founder of the Grytviken whaling station at South Georgia. In February 1903, Larsen lost the *Antarctic* to the ice in the strait since named for her. He led his crew of 20 men to Paulet, where they built a rock hut, froze a supply of seals and penguins, and overwintered, losing just one man.

Slowing, the *Ioffe* traces a zigzag course through crowding icebergs. Where the sound narrows, she slows again, feeling her way through the accumulated pack ice, as the snow, which has been falling since last night, comes swirling in again. The only life to be seen in the white world are pintado and snow petrels and Adélie penguins, which will be common as our ship moves farther south. The long-tailed black-and-white Adélie—the classic headwaiter penguin in white tie and tails—is also called the ice bird, for like the emperor, it is a true Antarctic endemic that never strays north of the South Orkneys and South Sandwiches. As the most polar of the three brush-tail penguins (the gentoo and the chin strap are its sibling species in the genus *Pygoscelis*), Adélies have shorter bills with longer feathers at the base for additional protection against cold.

Abandoning their waddle as the ship draws near, the Adélies flop onto their bellies. Pushed by stout legs set well to the rear, wing tips probing like ski poles, they churn rapidly over the ice, pour off the floes, and vanish through the looking glass of the black surface.

Working her way eastward through loose floes toward Erebus and Terror Gulf, which opens out into the Weddell Sea, the ship is buffeted by strong cold winds off the thousand miles and more of Weddell pack ice. The tumult of ice around Paulet Island may be fractured icebergs broken off and drifted northward from the Larsen Ice Shelf on this east side of the peninsula, which in January 1995 commenced a great cracking and collapse over the course of a few days. Although no direct cause has been determined, an indirect cause is assumed to be global warming.

With her limited ice-breaking capacity, our research vessel can work no closer than two miles from high rounded Paulet; we board the inflatables to search for leads through the drift ice and small bergs.

Three crab-eater seals, looking blond on the white snow, turn up their noses but seem otherwise indifferent, and the Adélie penguins that had fled before the uproar of a ship crashing through the ice pay little attention to our small craft. With the motor turned off, our boat drifts in close to the floes as two more crab-eaters slip beautifully along the blue-green edges. True Antarctic animals, crab-eaters are uncommon farther north; they breed on this snowy drift ice, often far from shore, where the insulation of their blubber, like the feather insulation of the penguins, keeps the snow from melting on the ice beneath them. Despite their name, the long, languorous animals, weighing up to 700 pounds, subsist mainly on krill. Usually encountered in small family groups, the crab-eater is the Earth's most abundant seal, with an estimated population of some 30 million.

The boats zigzag through the crowding ice. We are now close enough to Paulet's shore to breathe the sharp ammoniac smell of the huge penguin colony, but in the end, we are unable to find a way in between floes. The inshore current called the East Wind Drift, deflected into deep embayments such as the Weddell Sea, forms a clockwise gyre that masses ice along this eastern coast of the peninsula. The same current transported the icebound *Endurance* some 1,200 miles north and west from the point in the southwestern Weddell Sea where, in January 1914, she was beset in the ice pack at a point scarcely 20 miles from the continental shore and 85 miles from her destination on the south Weddell coast at Vahsel Bay. In early November, when the ice-stoved *Endurance* began her slow collapse, Ernest Shackleton led a reconnaissance party some 350 miles across the ice, seeking the solid rock of Paulet Island and the shelter of Carl Larsen's stone hut.

At the ship, I climb to the upper deck and stare away across the emptiness of ice, the wind biting my face. In the jagged waste of the Weddell Sea southeast of Paulet, black specks appear in my mind's eye from far out in the hallucinatory whiteness, hauling a lifeboat in their desperate advance toward terra firma. Unable to reach Paulet's shore due to pressure ridges from "growling impacting ice," the reconnaissance party from the *Endurance* return to the doomed ship, which after drifting for 281 days, was finally crushed by the shifting pack; she sank on November 21, 1914. With no faith in the shifting surface, the expedition dragged both of the ship's boats over hundreds of agonizing miles northwest to open water, where the boats were launched and rowed to Elephant Island, northwest of the peninsula—the only place that the *Endurance* crew set foot on Antarctic shores.

This afternoon, returning west, the ship coasts the north end of the Trinity Peninsula for several hours before drawing near the rust-red promontory called Brown Bluff. Adélies by the tens of thousands are scattered uphill in a dense spatter of white breasts from the tide line to the high bare gravel ridges. Since Adélies eat mostly *Euphausia* shrimp, small waves in the shallows are discolored by the pinkish spit-up of half-digested krill, which, together with copious wet guano, gives the windswept a sharp bad stink as well as a pinkish stain.

At Brown Bluff, we set foot on the continent for the first time. Making way on the beach, the penguins set up a terrific clamor, glaring at the intruders with mad stone-blue eyes. Others rocket from the shallow waves and carom off our boots, dodging through the human legs and scrambling up the beach. Clearly the birds fear us much less than they fear the predatory leopard seal, which patrols the shores of penguin colonies, snapping up stragglers as they come and go; seizing the penguin, the leopard may actually shake it inside out, leaving behind only the feathered skin. Though the leopard seal, too, subsists mainly on *Euphausia,* individuals have been reported with as many as 16 penguins in their stomachs.

Gangs of chicks loiter all along the beach among the adults, together with two dozen gentoos and a single chin strap. Today we are south of the northernmost range of the emperor penguin, which has been reported from this region, and so—although the chance is small—we scan the multitudes for what should look like a large pale king penguin with head markings less flame-colored than old gold. Since there are no kings in Antarctica to confuse a sighting, an emperor could be identified a long way off.

Continuing west across Hope Bay (where the Nordenskjöld party was stranded for the winter after the loss of the *Antarctic*) on her way to fetch them, the *Ioffe* passes Argentina's Esperanza Station, birthplace of the White Continent's first child. The baby was born in January 1978 to Silvia Morello de Palma, wife of the station commandant, who came here when seven months pregnant so that the birth might reinforce any territorial claim made by her country.

On the bridge in the late afternoon there is talk of the green flash, a mysterious and controversial phenomenon that intrigued the French writer Jules Verne (*Le Rayon Vert*). Where the sun sets on a clear ocean horizon, at an optimal distance of some 60 miles from the observer, it is said, an astonishing green light may be emitted by oxygen atoms. Most of us are skeptical. I have seen green-tinged sunset skies in the Gulf of Mexico and in Africa but have never witnessed anything that could be called a "flash." While open to the possibility, I am more than content with the mystery at hand—a luminous, prolonged, and quite extraordinary sunset without flash that fires the snow peaks of the offshore archipelago and the ice castles drifting slowly northward toward the Southern Ocean.

LIVINGSTON ISLAND

Over the night, our ship angles south across the strait to Hannah's Point on Livingston Island, the first site of Antarctic sealing; the *Hannah* was wrecked here in that first sealing season, on Christmas Day of 1820—a fate identical to that of the *Lady Troubridge* out of Liverpool, lost that same day off the east point of King George Island. (Unless one perceives it as nature's retribution for the bloody slaughter of the unsuspecting seals, it is hard not to attribute the coincidence of dates to the effects of Yuletide grog.) A few months later, the 11-man crew of *The Lord Melville* of London, shipwrecked not far away at Esther Harbor, became the first human beings—albeit inadvertently—to overwinter in Antarctica.[29]

At the head of the bay looms a vast glacier whose glistening ice cliffs extend for miles. In the morning sun, against high white walls, rise black gleaming backs of a pod of humpback whales, and chin strap penguins flip about among the boats as we go ashore. The chin strap colony on Hannah's Point has made room for scattered gentoos and a few macaronis; with their chrome yellow head plumes and fiery red eyes, the macaronis bustle officiously through the throng. The few nest scrapes this species has established in the colony may be the southernmost in all their range, which extends as far north as the Falklands and the coastal archipelago of southern Chile. Antarctic shags, kelp gulls, and sheathbills, perhaps expanding their distribution southward in the warming climate, breed here, too.

Hundreds of feet below the cliff rim, where I climb to enjoy the view, 49 elephant and a lone Weddell seal, tawny and light-spotted, lie hauled out on the black basalt pebbles of the beach. In this light, the big pinnipeds, fat and neckless, have a lustrous golden sheen. Between their warm velvets and a jade green sea, the surf spreads a delicate lace over the shining stones.

Astonishingly, this frigid sea with temperatures scarcely above freezing supports some 200 fish species and a full complement of invertebrate bottom life—crinoids, starfish, tunicates, worms, sponges, snails, and various crustaceans, in addition to the clouds of drifting krill. As at South Georgia, the marine food cycles depend largely on the crustacean *Euphausia superba*, the sole link in the food chain between the single-cell diatom that its larvae feed on and the huge blue whale, which may ingest four tons of it each day. Even a crab-eater may swallow down six tons each year. Thus one species essentially supports an estimated 85 million penguins and 80 million seabirds, together with thousands of pinnipeds and, until recent decades, the abounding whales, in what must have been the greatest concentration of marine wildlife in the world.

In the warming climate of this northwest region of the peninsula, chin straps and other more northerly animals, including the elephant seals on the black beach below, continue to displace creatures dependent on year-round ice such as Adélie penguins and the four endemic seals. (An adaptable invading species will always displace a more specialized endemic that is strictly dependent on a certain ecosystem.) That the krill-feeding chin straps and Adélies must forage ever farther from the coast appears to favor the chin straps, which like those we observed in the mid-ocean wastes hundreds of miles west of South Georgia and also west of the South Sandwich archipelago, are better adapted than the ice birds to the open sea. The warming trend has also brought increased precipitation in the form of snow, which can disrupt and even obliterate Adélie breeding colonies on the scattered points of exposed gravel they require.

Thus Adélie colonies, known from their layers of organic detritus to have been occupied for over 600 years, are being usurped by the southbound chin straps. Near the United States' Palmer station on King George Island, one Adélie colony has gone extinct each year since 1988; at Livingston Island, we would find no Adélies at all. Although still numerous at points all around the continent, the delightful ice birds seem to have begun a long decline.

GONDWANA LAND

Drift timbers collecting on the beach at Hannah's Point due to wind and currents are the first sign of man's works and days I have noticed in Antarctica, on shore or in the sea. Another is the small cache of fossils that earlier visitors have left behind on a large boulder out of respect for the environmental clause in the Antarctic Treaty that forbids the removal of natural objects, down to the humblest pebble, bone, or feather. The cache on the boulder includes fossil ferns and toothshells, petrified wood, and assorted shards of basalt, jasper, and green serpentine, spat up in fire from the inner Earth of 300 to 400 million years ago, when this continent was still joined to South America, Africa, India, and Australia, in that primordial landmass called Gondwana.

On a sealing expedition (1829-31) led by the American Nathaniel Palmer, a physician-naturalist named James Eights found carbonized wood on an exposed slope of King George Island, but the significance of Eights's find was not truly understood until more than 50 years later, in 1892-93, when the ubiquitous Captain Carl A. Larsen, on the ship *Jason,* exploring much of the Weddell Sea coast while hunting seals and whales, discovered fossil wood and leaves on Seymour Island—the first indisputable evidence that Antarctic Gondwana had a temperate to subtropical climate, fauna, and flora. In the Cretaceous period (circa 144 to 65 million years ago), the Gondwanan forests included tree ferns, cycads, palms, conifers, and deciduous trees, also freshwater fish, dinosaurs, and perhaps reptiles.

With its final separation from the southern continents around 25 million years ago, Antarctic Gondwana commenced its southward drift, increasingly cut off from temperate seas by the great circumpolar current. Eventually its ice cap began forming, but during interglacial periods, when the ice cap and most of its glaciers must have melted, these polar latitudes had a temperate climate with high rainfall and the warm, wet conditions required for reforestation. In 1902, at Seymour Island off the peninsula's east coast, Swedish geologist Otto Nordenskjöld, investigating the Weddell coast with Captain Larsen on the ill-fated *Antarctic,* would turn up the fossil of a giant penguin half again as large as the great emperor. Another fossil penguin, *Pachydptes ponderosus,* was the height of an average man and almost twice as heavy, at about 300 pounds. Since then, fossil footprints of a raptor over ten feet high have been found on King George Island—"probably ... the so-called terror bird, a flightless, fast-running relative of the cranes and rails. Its clawed feet enabled it to disembowel mammals, including the two-meter-long glyptodonts, which were armored like armadillos. Terror birds probably originated in South America. At the time of the closure of the Darien Gap, 2.5 million years ago, they were the largest carnivores in South America."[30]

The last of Antarctica's terrestrial life would perish in the last Ice Age, as the frozen continent disappeared beneath its ice sheet. A few minute woody plants, the relics of a once widespread and various flora, persisted longer, but eventually the formation of the ice would scour away or bury all but a few traces of fossil evidence. The confirmation of Gondwana's ancient life was finally worked out by comparing its few traces with comparable fossils from the departed continents.[31] In 1985, some ancient wood was identified as *Nothofagus* or "southern beech," leaves, roots, and all; this genus still dominates the forests of Tierra del Fuego, and occurs as well in New Zealand, southern Australia, and Tasmania.

Although fossil evidence of small dinosaurs and early mammals such as marsupials has now turned up, Antarctica's isolation by the polar oceans over millions of years of southward movement, its accumulating ice and drastic climate change, would put an end to all vertebrate terrestrial life, in one of the greatest natural extinctions in Earth history. On the few small edges not encased in ice, life is limited to a few tiny invertebrates such as lice and mites, springtails and midges. Similarly, the flora was reduced from variegated forest to low tundra plants and grasses, as in South Georgia, and finally, the few fragile lichens and mosses that subsist here and there on rocks and bones in the dry deserts and along the coast. Even here in this northern region of the peninsula, well north of the Antarctic Circle, the only surviving vascular plants are a mosslike cushion plant with tiny white-green blossoms and a hairgrass that forms a similar hemispheric clump to ward off desiccation by the cold, dry wind.

DECEPTION ISLAND

At Livingston Island, toward noon, we return to the boats at the far end of the long beach and head offshore toward the ship. The wind and seas have been building since early morning, and once again, approaching the ship, the boats encounter a strong surge of six- to eight-foot waves. The *Ioffe* is obliged to spin her stern, placing her hull broadside to the wind with the gangway in the lee before the skilled crewmen, grasping each passenger by the upper and lower arm, can impel them on the upsurge leap onto the platform. Once all are safely back aboard, wind and sea almost immediately subside.

Nine miles south of Hannah's Point is Deception Island, an isolated volcanic mount some 60 miles west of the mainland. On its outside wall at Baily Head, on layered cliffside rocks, is a huge chin strap colony estimated at 180,000 birds. As at Brown Bluff, the heavy sprinkle of white bird breasts on the reddish slopes is visible from several miles offshore, since the colony has expanded from black basalt pebbles on the beach up the steep scree slope to the old volcano rim, hundreds of feet above—an astonishing climb for small waddling pedestrians driven only by the need to pump a gulletful of softened krill into their chicks.

At first sight, Deception seems to be just another island "of ice and black basalt, now and then tinged russet or blue by oozings of iron or copper," as it is described in *The Crystal Desert*, an excellent book about this region of the Peninsula. But south of Baily Head, the gaunt Cathedral Crags mark the mouth of Neptune's Bellows, a narrow portal through high cliffs that leads to the "deception" of the island's name, a hidden anchorage in the sheltered basin of a huge caldera seven miles across. All around, the steep walls of the collapsed volcano rise to the rim from which, in 1820, the American sealer Nathaniel Palmer of Stonington, Connecticut, who discovered the caldera, claimed a sighting of the continental peaks of the Trinity Peninsula, 60 miles away to the southeast—a distinct possibility in such clear air.

A better claimant may have been Captain Thaddeus von Bellingshausen, who earlier that year had sailed closer to the continent for a longer period than anyone before him. On February 2, 1820, Bellingshausen recorded, "[W]e hauled close to the wind on a south-east course and had made two miles in this direction when we observed that there was a solid stretch of ice running from east through south and west." This ice wall was close enough to ascertain that "its edge was perpendicular and formed into little coves, whilst the surface sloped upwards toward the south to a distance so far that its end was out of sight even from the masthead." And subsequently he mentions "ice-covered mountains," sighted farther down the coast.[32] These sightings, scarcely three weeks after Bransfield sighted the Trinity Peninsula at the north end of Graham Land, are generally accepted as "the first discovery of the main Antarctic continent."[33]

Continuing eastward and mapping the South Shetlands, the Russian mariner arrived at Deception Island, which, almost from the day of its discovery the year before, had become the leading sealing and whaling harbor in Antarctica. Bellingshausen encountered 18 British and American sealing vessels, one of them captained by Nathaniel Palmer, who came aboard the Russian vessel.[34] According to a putative witness, American sealing captain Edmund Fanning in his *Voyages Round the World,* and also, more fancifully, by Palmer's niece, a Mrs. Loper, in a 1907 paper, Bellingshausen verified Palmer's claim to a first sighting of the continent from Deception's rim and had furthermore named it "Palmer's Land" in his honor. Alas, Captain

Bellingshausen, while recalling their brief meeting, fails to verify this historic moment in his journal.

In England, of course, the continent's discoverer was Captain Bransfield, shoring up the Admiralty claim to preeminence in Antarctic exploration established in the previous century by Captain Cook. In 1908, Britain claimed Deception Island as part of its Falkland Island Dependency. Together with Port Lockroy, farther south, it was occupied in 1944 by the Royal Navy as a base for monitoring German activity in the Drake Passage. It was finally abandoned after two large eruptions (1967 and 1969) caused mudslides that threatened its air station (and the Argentine and Chilean stations, too). The eruptions are symptoms of tectonic spreading of the Earth's crust that is widening the Bransfield Strait and moving the South Shetlands farther west into the Pacific.

Since the entrance appears less than a quarter mile across, ships must take pains to avoid submerged ledges and the wreck of the British whaler *Southern Hunter,* which ran aground here in 1957 while attempting to escape the attention of an Argentine Navy vessel off the coast. We anchor just north of the entrance in Whaler's Bay, site of the Mekla Whaling Station, abandoned in 1933. Across the caldera rise volcanic cones, one of which erupted less than 30 years ago, creating waves that destroyed the jetty and much of the old station and flooded out the whalers' cemetery.

Due to volcanic hot springs and their gases, the bowl is almost free of snow and ice, and what snow remains on the farther rims is thin and dirty. Though grasses are lacking, the bowl shelters mosses, lichens, and a few small insects. The far-flung birds out of the north that occasionally turn up here have included the lovely upland sandpiper from North America.

Today the Mekla station is reduced to wind-scoured ruins of old sheds and barracks, rusty oil tanks, and skeletons of whales and boats. The decrepit British Antarctic Survey hangar once housed the seaplane of the Australian aviator Sir Hubert Wilkins, who made the first flights across Antarctica in the late twenties and early thirties; Wilkins would complain to the American ornithologist Robert Cushman Murphy that those damnable seabirds drawn to the whaling operations were imperiling his approach and landing.

BY EVENING, the ship is well south of the South Shetlands. On the sea horizon, the slowly sinking sun is brilliantly reflected by the towers and plateaus of stately icebergs, white and blue. An hour later, the icebergs are all gone; there is only empty ocean out to westward. The star that is our sun has lost the violence of its burning, and from the bridge, I watch it through binoculars in order to observe the precise moment when the fireball first touches the horizon. At the touch, a strange suspense grows, for the sea appears impenetrable, halting the sun's descent behind its planet. An instant later, our star turns a brilliant molten gold, an igneous, unearthly gold, which instead of setting, melts to an oblong ellipse that flows outward along the horizon line like mercury.

Astonished, I urge a passenger who has come out on the bridge to look directly at the sun through his binoculars. Thinking I've gone mad, he cries, "But it won't blind me?" Told rudely to hurry, he raises his binoculars in time to see that unimaginable burning. As if by wand, its astonishing incandescence is transformed from purest molten gold into an emerald fire so radiant and fierce as to transcend color entirely; it pierces my brain as if to strike me blind. In the same hallucinatory moment, it winks out, vanishing down behind the curve of Earth.

I hear the loud gasp of the passenger and doubtless I gasp, too. Others on the outside deck at the far end of the bridge have also glimpsed it, for there comes a low murmur of awe—the gratitude and joy one feels in the presence of anything so immediate and yet transcendent. Perhaps mystery might be intuited as that last element of wild nature that still eludes the curiosity of man.

Lines about something quite else by the excellent American poet James Wright convey the eerie sense of what we saw, though I cannot say just why:

> A cloister, a silence,
> closing around a blossom of fire.
> When I stand upright in the wind,
> my bones turn to dark emerald.[35]

That unholy emerald fire, gone without a trace, was replaced by an ordinary—which is to say, merely extraordinary—Antarctic sunset, as soft sky blue turned to a faint soft lavender. There it remained, for the evening was still clear, clear, clear, with no oncoming dusk. The night never grew dark enough to reveal the Southern Cross nor even that boundless constellation known as the Magellanic Clouds.[36]

THE CONTINENT

The ship is on a southeast course toward Graham Land on the peninsula, which rises in a long line of ice mountains. The knowledge that farther to the south, whole ranges with peaks higher than these lie entirely submerged beneath vast plateaus of ice, is profoundly stirring. I had never quite comprehended that this mighty realm, half again as large as Europe, has an average elevation almost twice as high as Asia, in part because there is no low-lying land: The ice that covers all but 2 percent of it, in fact, averages more than a mile and a half deep. At first sight, one understands at once why Terra Australis Incognita is the last untrodden wilderness on the planet.

The West Antarctic Ice Sheet, separated by the Transantarctic Mountains from the far larger, higher, and much colder Ice Cap of East Antarctica, was formed perhaps 20 million years ago; it has been shrinking for 10 million years and has already lost two-thirds of its mass, raising world sea levels by more than 30 feet. In recent years, it has been suggested that the ice sheet disintegrated about 400,000 years ago, reformed itself, and could now be repeating this cycle, to judge from the ongoing collapse of the Larsen Ice Shelf and other symptoms of instability and change. Indeed, the whole sheet, anchored at present on the ancient Precambrian bedrock below sea level, might one day slide away into the ocean.

The ongoing rise in temperatures recorded in West Antarctica, especially here in the northwestern peninsula, is mostly related by research station scientists to world climate change. Attributed by almost everyone except kept scientists of the energy and automotive industries (and the servants of industry in high public office) to heat-trapping carbon dioxide and related emissions generated by fossil fuels, global warming has become an urgent long-term threat to coastal cities and communities, world weather patterns and economies, and environmental welfare—in short, the future.

Having witnessed the impact of climate change on such regions as the Alaskan Arctic, the old kingdom of Lo north of the Himalaya, and the equatorial mountains of East Africa—not to speak of my own small property in New York State, where southern bird species moving ever farther north have been displacing certain local species for a good half century—I am now witnessing it on the Antarctic Peninsula, where shorelines are emerging as the glaciers decline: The peninsula's Marr Glacier is retreating more than 30 feet each year, even as the ocean drift ice withdraws southward and birds and mammals from the north establish residence.

According to scientists, this northwestern peninsula, with the Bellingshausen Sea to westward, is one of three geographic regions of the Earth most affected by rapid warming. A second is located in north-central Siberia and a third in that region of northwest North America and the Beaufort Sea that includes the beautiful Arctic National Wildlife Refuge, long coveted by fossil fuelers for development despite its shrinking oil reserves, high cost of extraction, and the fatal disruption of the Earth's last stronghold of Ice Age mammals that drilling in the permafrost—already melting—must inevitably cause.[37] (The melting permafrost releases vast amounts of methane, increasing "greenhouse gas" accumulation in the atmosphere.) Arctic sea ice has decreased by 40 percent in less than 30 years, as the North Pole becomes increasingly surrounded by open water, and glaciers retreat almost everywhere on Earth except East Antarctica.

Analysis of sediments and other evidence suggests that the rapidity of warming in the northern peninsula is probably unmatched over the last two millennia. Its average temperature has risen 5°F in the last 50 years, about ten times the average rise worldwide; its winter temperatures, rising twice as fast as anywhere on Earth in the past century, include an alarming 10°F rise on this west side of the peninsula in the half century since 1950 alone. In consequence, over the past 30 years, its season of annual melt has lengthened by about three weeks.

It is now feared that the whole West Antarctic Ice Sheet has been sliding downhill into the sea since the last Ice Age, or about 11,000 years. In the past half century alone, seven ice shelves have collapsed, a phenomenon at least partly attributable to rising sea levels and storms made worse by climate change. At present, the Larsen Ice Shelf, which lies perhaps 30 miles east of our ship's present position, across the peninsular mountains on the Weddell Sea, is fracturing and splitting off plateaus of ice that are comparable in area to whole small nations. The collapse of floating shelves such as the Larsen would not cause a rise in sea level any more than ice cubes melting in a drink, but since the shelves are the outer areas of the ice flowing down from the high interior, any sudden dissolution might release the glaciers to descend faster to the sea, causing a rise in ocean levels all around the world.[38]

The precise pattern of events that causes such drastic change remains elusive, and no one can predict with much assurance how long the present warming will continue. Some scientists doubt that "global warming" is separable from the warming trend between the last Ice Age and the present; others suggest that ice shelves might actually *grow* because of the increased precipitation and ice formation brought by the warming.[39] Whatever the explanation, there seems no doubt that West Antarctica's climate is unstable, and that an ongoing temperature increase, upsetting some balance not yet understood, may precipitate a melting, followed by a sudden catastrophic rise in sea levels around the world.

If even a small part of the Ice Cap were to melt, world sea levels would rise from several feet to several yards, inundating most coasts. (If the whole Ice Cap were to melt, as it has in past ages, sea levels around the world would rise an estimated 260 feet, destroying a number of low-lying countries.) Since sea levels have risen only eight and a half inches in the past century, the three-foot rise projected by the year 2080 is serious enough. Many millions will become refugees, depopulating the long U.S. coasts up to 50 miles inland, including all of southern Florida and the Mississippi Delta, also much of Bangladesh, the Philippines, Southeast Asia, the coasts of Africa, and innumerable Pacific atolls.[40]

SOUTHWARD

The *Ioffe* proceeds south and west through the white world to the Palmer Archipelago and the broad Gerlache Strait, named for Baron Adrien de Gerlache de Gomery, leader of a Belgian expedition to Graham Land in 1898; besides Lieutenant de Gerlache, those aboard the *Belgica* included Polish geologist Henryk Arctowski, ship's doctor

Frederick Cook (a veteran of Robert Peary's North Greenland expedition of 1892), and first mate Roald Amundsen, age 25, a young Norwegian just returned from a sealing voyage to the Arctic aboard Captain Carl A. Larsen's *Jason* as part of his obsessive preparations for a life of polar travel and exploration. Amundsen had already learned much from the experience of his countryman Fridtjof Nansen, who in crossing the Greenland Ice Cap in 1888, had established the importance of light sledges and sled dogs, skis, Inuit clothing, and even tents and cooking utensils adapted to light swift polar travel. Eventually *Belgica,* beset in the ice, spent the winter drifting west across the Bellingshausen Sea; she was spared disaster mostly because of Frederick Cook, whose experience and leadership were to save an ill-conceived expedition from itself. Indeed Dr. Cook, in Amundsen's opinion, was "the one man of unfaltering courage, unfailing hope, endless cheerfulness, and unwearied kindness"—a view intriguingly at variance with his subsequent reputation. Cook would be vilified a few years later as a false claimant to the first climb of Alaska's Mount McKinley, then the conquest of the North Pole, and later still would be imprisoned for common fraud.

Between Cuverville Channel and the Arctowski Peninsula, our ship penetrates the ice escarpments, up to 3,000 feet high, of the magnificent Errera Channel, five and a half miles long. Scattered snow petrels are the only birds observed in this snow passage, as they were between the towering white walls of South Georgia's Drygalski Fjord. What can explain the affinity of these lovely apparitions for these snow canyons that seem to lack any other sign of life?

Beyond the channel, three humpbacks blow and sink away again, and a few crab-eaters turn slowly with their floes. Beyond the crab-eaters, what looks at first like a mud ridge on the ice catches a cold gleam of sun—the leopard seal. It is too lump-headed, large, and long to be anything else. Though the leopard sieves krill, it also eats fish, carrion, and penguins, and may pursue the young of smaller seals. The leopard seal is not known to attack human beings; on the other hand, it has rarely had the opportunity. Captain Cook's crew had a brush with a hungry leopard, and Dr. Carleton Ray, a marine biologist with considerable scuba experience beneath Antarctic ice, once told me that Antarctic divers are very leery of it.

Birds are few in these colder waters farther south, but minke and humpback seem ever more numerous, slicing the black water sheen between the floes. The minke is an orca-size, dark gray animal with white flanks, long jaws, and the small curved dorsal that distinguishes the swift rorqual whales. One minke that passed under the port bow, perhaps 12 feet down, showed the long gleam of its white underside as it rolled to inspect the vessel's hull, outlined like a great whale on the silver surface.

The emperor penguin breeds south of these latitudes in the Weddell and Ross Seas, and intermittently along the continent's outer coast, and there is also a small colony at tiny Dion Island, farther south on the peninsula. Thus, a sighting remains an exciting possibility, since an occasional juvenile from Dion strays north on the drifting pack; we keep an eye out for the one Antarctic bird we have not seen.

Andvord Bay and Neko Harbor, walled around by snow peaks, cut eastward from this Pacific side of the peninsula to a point only 25 miles overland from the Larsen Ice Shelf on the Weddell Sea. At Neko, packed tumulus descends from the broad snowfields and an ice blue sky, and the bedrock of the lost continent peeps out from beneath its tomb of ice, exposing more stone and gravel every year. The ship anchors in a cove not far from an overhanging glacier where snowbanks show the reddish tinge of a snow algae.

Under the glacier, the cove water is so clear that hunting gentoos can be seen scooting along beneath the surface, rowing their flippers with quick strokes like water beetles, their strong, horny feet serving as rudders. All are fascinated by the scooting penguins, shooting back and forth in the clear water almost at our feet, and one merry person, as if seeking to emulate them, scoots on the snowy ice and glides down to the water's edge on her bottom.

Like most penguin species, gentoos are dark above and white below. Since little of the body is ever visible above the surface, the crests, color, and patterns that identify them to other penguins as well as to human admirers are all located on or about the head.

All penguins have short-necked streamlined shapes that appear thick in the middle, like tuna fish and footballs. All have fused spines and straight legs without joints, and the legs are set back farther on the body than in flying birds, which accounts for the upright stance; they lack undulation even when they swim. Similarly, the flat aero-dynamic wings, fused at wrist and elbow, hang straight down, since they cannot be tucked or folded. Unlike true flightless birds such as the emu and the moa, this family has retained the keel or "breastbone" of the flying birds, since their powerful wings require a strong mus-cle structure for "flying" underwater. Oddly, the strongest wing stroke underwater is upward and forward rather than back and down.

The penguins developed flightlessness and weight in order to exploit a new ecological niche beyond the reach of other diving species. No longer needing the light hollow skeletons of flying birds, they formed solid bones and heavy layers of subcutaneous fat, pro-viding the ballast needed for deepwater feeding (they may even swal-low stones). Larger species such as the king penguin and the emperor may descend some 700 feet below the surface, where a heavy rib cage is required to withstand the pressure.

Penguin flightlessness might never have evolved without the swarming food available in the Southern Ocean, and also a climate and terrain too cold and barren for terrestrial predators such as weasels, bears, and foxes, which in the north confined the nesting of the flight-less great auk to offshore rocks and islets. Here on the northern peninsula, there are only avian predators—kelp gulls, skuas, giant-petrels, and the sheathbill—none of them larger than the adults of most penguin species. As we journey south, only skuas remain to prey on eggs and chicks of nesting penguins, though leopard seals and occa-sionally an orca may await them at the ice edge.

The gentoos at Neko are monitored by the brass eyes of the skuas, which nest on a rock knoll overlooking the colony, and I am grimly monitored as well. In late morning, for the first time in more than a half century of observing seabird rookeries, I am struck hard on the crown by a swooping bird. The South Polar skua is large, short-necked, and powerful, with a stout hooked beak, and its blow actually staggers me and sends my watch cap flying; that wool cap may have saved me a near scalping. Though I muster a grin, I am chagrined, since the bird had warned me with screeching dives that were only turned away at the last moment by careless waves of my hand over my head.

During the three hours spent onshore, the small glacier has calved repeatedly, with ominous grumblings and sharp cracks and thunder; fractured ice comes avalanching down into the cove. When a loud crack resounds as our returning boat draws near the ship, the alert helmsman turns her bow into the sudden surge, which lifts and shatters the carpet of drift ice between boat and glacier and slaps a cold wave ten feet high against the *Ioffe*'s hull.

Crossing the strait to Anvers Island, which rises over 9,000 feet to Mount Français, the ship turns southwest down Neumayer Channel. At Wiencke Island (named for a Norwegian seaman on the *Belgica* expedition who washed overboard and vanished), a party prepares to go ashore at the British station called Port Lockroy, where humpbacks and minkes rise in silence under the white mountains.[41]

Someone has seen a leopard seal slip off a floe not 50 yards from the ship as she was anchoring. With two of our birders, I run to the stern, following the big liverish seal with binoculars as it hunts east among the snowy cakes, reptilian head held high out of the water. Eventually it flips out onto a floe. The leopard, up to 11 feet long, may attain a weight of about 1,200 pounds, nearly twice the weight of an adult crab-eater, and this one appears to be stalking a young crab-eater that lies behind a snow ridge on that floe. The leopard slips back into the water and circles the floe, popping its head up several times as if to scare the smaller seal before swimming on about its business.

THE BLACK TWIN PEAKS of Cape Renard form the dramatic entrance to Lemaire Channel, a four-mile passage through the towering white walls between Booth Island and Mount Cloos on the peninsula. Where the channel narrows to less than a half mile, the snow masses are reflected in the black mirror of the glassy surface—glassy because protected from the wind in an ice canyon, which is surely one of the loveliest places I have ever seen.

South of the channel, four leopard seals are hauled out on the ice at discrete and discreet distances from one another; like many predators, they tend to be solitary. One of these is passed so close that the black "leopard" spots in the throat area as well as larger blotches on the dark brown pelage of the back are clearly visible. A distinct neck, uncommon among seals, separates its head from its long, sinuous body. When it turns to observe the passing ship, its flattish crown and flared wide nostrils and long mouth evoke the snout of a moray eel or python, viewed head on, and the elongated underjaw line, extending back beyond the sunken eye, curls up in a disconcerting sort of smile.

A low ridge of bare granite rock with a small Adélie colony is Petermann Island,[42] and south of Petermann is a wide reach of open water where a company of city-block-size icebergs, frost white and cerulean blue, have composed themselves in a fantastical modern metropolis. In front of an alabaster ice face with blue grottos, a pair of humpbacks, blowing mightily, sounds and rises, shouldering up waves.

For the next two hours, the humpbacks tolerate the close approach of the small boats. Thirty yards away and then much closer, a huge barnacled black head thrusts straight up through the surface to inspect us—the so-called spy-hopping, also a habit of the orca. The humpbacks indulge us, erupting suddenly alongside with thick guttural puffs like small waves washing onto a shell beach, then sinking vertically, leaving behind a moist and stinking mist of cetacean plumbing. So close does one come that a voice cries out, "We're going to die!"

As conservation biologist Roger Payne reminds us in his excellent *Among Whales,* the humpback is astonishingly forbearing in man's presence, considering our centuries-old slaughter of this animal, which was one of the first species to receive protection (we see more of them than we do other great whales because of their inshore feeding habit). Even so, they grow weary of our company. Arching broad backs, hoisting huge flukes high in the air, they slip soundlessly into the deeps, leaving a faint redolence of whales in the clarion air among the silent monuments.

Two more feeding closer to the ship are indifferent to our approach, neither sounding nor moving away when the boat draws near. Though humpbacks migrate north to breed in temperate waters, they spend four months engulfing food in the Antarctic during this summer season when the breeding krill drift together in vast clouds. The whales accumulate sufficient fat to maintain themselves during those long months in northern waters when sieving the scattered plankton is so inefficient that the huge beasts scarcely deign to feed at all. We have had fine luck with humpback whales and minkes and exciting observations of every Antarctic seal except the rare Ross seal of the dense pack ice farther south (which after it was first observed on James Clark Ross's British Antarctic Expedition of 1839 would scarcely be seen again for a hundred years).

Near the Argentine Islands, at 65° 15 minutes south latitude, the *Ioffe* slows to alter course. We shall not cross the Antarctic Circle less than a hundred miles away, a failure made more disappointing by the knowledge that Captain Cook, "pestered" by ice, crossed it three times under sail. Just after midday, Captain Nikolai Apekhtin orders his helmsman to take a westward bearing down the Grandidier Channel toward the open ocean.

To escape the drift ice and massed bergs clotted around the peninsula and its islands, our ship clears the coastal archipelagoes entirely. The white mountains and the last polar birds fall gradually astern as she heads west toward the Bellingshausen Sea. Turning north that afternoon, she passes offshore of Smith Island, named for that uncelebrated William Smith who discovered the South Shetlands in 1819. Late in the long polar evening, at 62° south latitude, she is west of the South Shetlands on a northwest-by-north bearing, bound for Cape Horn.

NORTHWARD

The sea is smooth and foggy, with long, gentle swells, but we pay attention when the bridge reports storm warnings. Mariners are ever wary of the notorious Drake Passage where the southern Pacific and Atlantic Oceans meet and mix. The officers recall one northward leg when the *Ioffe*, laboring through enormous waves, was deluged for most of the voyage by the tons of water that broke over her bow.

However, the seas are moderate next morning as the ship enters an empty ocean plain devoid of icebergs, whales, and pelagic birds. As if the wind here in the Pacific were too light for gliding, or the plankton had thinned out for want of ice, I saw no petrels, only a solitary black-browed albatross in the ocean distance.

The ship is traversing the West Wind Drift, whose depth and width, spanning the latitudes, make it the mightiest of currents, with a volume equivalent to all of the Earth's rivers 135 times over. Before Tierra del Fuego split away from the Antarctic Peninsula, the main ocean currents flowed north and south between the Equator and the polar latitudes: The opening of this great strait under our hull impelled the Southern Ocean through the rift and eastward, into polar orbit.

Next day, the sea is misty and still tranquil, with long rolling swells. The absence of wind behind these mists is almost eerie. Peale's dolphins[43] in their elegant pattern of gray, black, and white roll up under the bows and shoot away again. All morning the gale birds reappear—wandering and royal albatrosses, white-chinned petrels, and the little blue-gray whalebirds, spinning through the sunny haze over the wake. Far out to westward, a small pod of great whales blows on the surface—finbacks, to judge from the spout, which I have seen off the beach on my home coast (a huge finback skull I discovered in the surf about ten years ago guards my front door). I am quietly excited, since each hour without storm improves our chance of a clear landfall at Cape Horn.

The weather holds. Toward one o'clock, the ship sights the southernmost tip of the great mountain range that extends almost unbroken from this point north through the Americas to the Arctic Circle and on across northern Alaska to the Bering Strait. The sense of such earthly distances, of time and geologic change, is profoundly moving, if only to put life into perspective. On deck, I lean against the bulkhead in contentment as the separate islands of the Cape take shape—Isla Hornos itself, then Cathedral Rocks and Isla Hermite, to the west and north. As a courtesy to his passengers, I suspect, Captain Nikolai is approaching South America from the Pacific side, perhaps a mile west of the Cape, so that when the ship turns eastward, she will "round the Horn."

Shearwaters, skuas, and blue-eyed cormorants crisscross the burly rock face of Isla Hornos, which appears to be about 200 feet high; two red-white navigation lights shine on the headland. Cape Horn is the side of an old crater wall, for as the ship passes, a caldera takes form behind the rim.

To the north, mysterious volcanos come and go in deep black cloud and shadows. To the northeast lies Isla Deceit, doubtless the site of some fatal trick of wind or tide that betrayed an old-time navigator. The perils of the Horn, the treacherous currents and murderous winds, have been legendary since 1578, when this headland was first rounded by Sir Francis Drake. For sailing ships, such waters might be perilous even on a calm day such as this one, with a wind too light to fill the sails and the becalmed vessel losing ground as the current sweeps her east along this coast toward Cape Agulheras, the Needles, a line of jagged rocks like broken teeth.

From the outermost rocks of Agulheras comes a swift flock of small birds, turning and bending tight over the wake, hurrying close up under the stern. Excited cries alert the scattered birders, for these are unmistakably Baird's sandpipers, which breed in the Arctic from eastern Siberia to Point Barrow in Alaska and Baffin Island in northeastern Canada. As if unfulfilled by a southward migration of 8,000 miles, the little birds have carried on past land's end; they are already three miles south of South America and going strong toward Antarctica, with hundreds of miles of open ocean still to cross.

Baird's sandpiper is familiar to the birder's, since it turns up in Texas in spring migration and appears in fall on my own Atlantic coast. The sense of the immense journey undertaken by these seven-inch creatures twice each year brings elation to this sighting, as if, in this moment, one had tapped into an extraordinary life force. Yet I am relieved when the flock rounds the ship and hurries back toward shore, for storms are still predicted for the Southern Ocean. It is February now, and the restless band will soon depart on its northward migration to the Arctic.

Gazing after the small wayfarers, we grin—no need to speak. The prospect of Cape Horn, so long awaited, then the sighting of these wind birds far from home—that's quite enough.

In misty sun on a soft gray sea, the ship passes a mile south of the Needles. Soon she alters course, bearing northeast and then due north again: She will reach the Beagle Channel after dark and set us ashore tomorrow morning at Ushuaia.

The longing for the Ice, the sadness of departure ...
it is as if I cannot after all bear to leave
this bleak waste of ice, glaciers, cold and toil.
—ERNEST SHACKLETON

At the same time that we are anxious
to explore and learn all things,
we require that all things be mysterious
and unexplorable.
—HENRY DAVID THOREAU

part two

THE LONGING
FOR THE ICE

OUR VOYAGE TO SOUTH GEORGIA and the Peninsula is over—
"one of the five best trips I ever made," says Victor Emanuel, who has
led over a hundred to places near and far across the world. "We saw
so *much!*" It's true: We are amply rewarded and fulfilled. And yet there
is a sense of something missing or unfinished, if only because we failed
to see the emperor penguin.

In any case, we are already discussing with the Batemans a return
to Antarctica from the far side of the world. Setting out from Tasmania,
we would voyage nearly a thousand miles to Macquarie Island, a sub-
Antarctic stronghold of marine birds and mammals about halfway to
the outer boundary of the Ross Sea ice. Sailing a month earlier in the
season and forging much farther south, we shall certainly find the
quintessential bird of the Antarctic, and not some lone juvenile, either,
but a raucous and colorful breeding colony of adults and half-grown
chicks. There is also the chance we might come across one of those two
exciting mammals we had missed on the first journey, the Southern
Ocean orca and the rarely seen Ross seal.

After so many years of Antarctic reading, I am eager to visit the
region of James Clark Ross's epochal discoveries, including the live
volcano that he named Mount Erebus and the daunting ramparts of
the Great Barrier, a vast ice plateau at the south end of the Ross Sea

that forbade farther navigation toward the Pole and thus became the starting point for most polar expeditions of the late 19th and early 20th centuries—the so-called "heroic age" of Antarctic exploration.

In 1820, off the icebound mainland coast west of the Peninsula, Thaddeus von Bellingshausen would record an "unusually large" penguin, three feet high and 59 pounds in weight, with cuttlefish beaks and pebbles in its stomach. In 1839, along the coast of what is now Adélie Land, a very large greenish-ivory egg of unknown provenance was found by a French expedition under the command of Captain Jules-Sébastien-César Dumont d'Urville. The large unknown bird killed by Bellingshausen's crew, and also the first custodian of that greenish-ivory egg brought back by the Dumont d'Urville expedition would turn out to be emperor penguins, but the species was first scientifically collected by the British Antarctic Expedition under Ross, whose gifted botanist and assistant surgeon Joseph Dalton Hooker secured a few specimens in the Ross Sea—the first "great penguins" ever brought back from Terra Australis Incognita for the enlightenment of the Known World.

The Ross expedition laid the groundwork for scientific study of Antarctica. Unlike the pious Captain Fitzroy on the *Beagle,* who in the same era, in the name of God, disapproved of Charles Darwin's scientific inquiries, Captain Ross shared Hooker's intense zeal for new knowledge and made space for his scientific labors in his own cabin. A friend of Darwin and his scientific ally, this man would become the eminent Sir Joseph Hooker, Britain's great botanical authority. In the last years of the nineties in the British Museum, Sir Joseph would encounter Dr. Edward Wilson, who was doing research for Robert Falcon Scott's *Discovery* expedition of 1901-1904. It is pleasant to think that Dr. Wilson might have inspected those earliest specimens of

A. forsteri with their collector standing at his shoulder: The species had gone unreported for some 60 years. In 1902, the *Discovery* expedition would locate the first known emperor colony on Ross Island, establishing the identity of Dumont d'Urville's enigmatic egg by comparing it with its own Ross Island specimens.

As an obsessed amateur naturalist since early boyhood, I had been delighted to discover in that Galway summer years ago that Cherry-Garrard's "worst journey in the world" referred not to the terrible saga of Scott and his polar party—although that, too, is wonderfully evoked—but to a brutal trek east to Cape Crozier from the Scott base on the west end of Ross Island in search of the eggs of the emperor penguin. The journey was led by the remarkable Dr. Wilson, born in 1872 to a family of ornithologist-physicians, who would serve on Scott's Antarctic expeditions as doctor scientist, ornithologist, artist, and confidant to both officers and men.

On a sledge reconnaissance to Cape Crozier on Ross Island, 1st Officer Charles Royds and 1st Engineer Reginald Skelton, peering down from an 800-foot cliff where "the snout of Cape Crozier" plunged into the Ross Sea, had seen live dots on the ice of a small bay where the cape escarpment met the white wall of the Barrier. A blizzard forbade investigation until five days later, when the young officers descended the cliffs into a flock of some 400 birds, including 30 living chicks and about 80 dead ones. Finding no eggs to bring back to Wilson (who was particularly interested in emperor embryology), they salvaged three dead chicks and a few eggshells. Dr. Wilson spent his final day in camp sketching and describing these poor scraps before departing with Scott and Merchant Marine officer Ernest Shackleton on the first overland trek toward the South Pole.

Like every man on the *Discovery* expedition, Royds and Skelton revered "Uncle Bill" Wilson, and seeing his excitement over their find, Royds returned to the emperor colony in early November, doubtless intending to collect live chicks, only to find that the ice cracked away and the colony departed, leaving one egg intact, abandoned in the snow. Dissecting this momentous egg on his return from the failed polar journey, Wilson found to his chagrin that its embryo was too far developed to be of use for scientific study.

The *Discovery,* beset in the ice, had to winter over. Hoping to find eggs less advanced, Wilson left for Cape Crozier on September 7 of the following year (1903), leading Royds and four crewmen with two sledges of gear and rations on the 67-mile journey over the frozen sea. On the fast ice at the foot of steep glaciated cliffs, he collected eight eggs, two live chicks, and more dead ones from a colony of about a thousand birds. But these eggs, too, were well advanced— strong evidence that this penguin's incubation must begin in late June or early July, in the dead of the Antarctic winter, which in turn suggested an extraordinary breeding cycle quite unlike anything known in other birds.

To take chicks at a later stage of growth, he returned to the colony in October, a compulsive and finally unproductive journey. "Those journeys to Cape Crozier were pretty average uncomfortable even for the Antarctic," Wilson wrote his father. "It has been worth doing—I feel that; but I'm not sure I could stand it all over again." Wilson knew enough to dread the winter journey that now seemed unavoidable, for Crozier was "a focus for wind and storm where every breath is converted, by the configuration of Mounts Erebus and Terror, into a regular drifting blizzard full of snow."

Returning to England in 1904, Wilson prepared his scientific papers, with special attention to *Aptenodytes forsteri,* the name given the bird after the Ross expedition. "I want my monograph on the Emperor Penguin to be a classic," he confided to his father in a rare expression of ambition to achieve scientific excellence. Many who knew Wilson's work in the field would confirm his painstaking observation, impeccable data, and rare artistic talent, not only in his species drawings but in camp and shipboard sketches and landscape watercolors. In November 1905, Sir Joseph Hooker, now 88, went to see the London exhibition of Wilson's work. "They are marvelous in numbers, interest, and execution," wrote Hooker, who had known these species at first hand in Antarctica. "The heads and bodies of the birds are the perfection of ornithological drawing and colouring. They are absolutely alive."

In 1911, as chief scientific officer on Scott's second expedition, Wilson was still speculating that the emperor might be "the nearest approach to a primitive form not only of a penguin but of a bird," and even, perhaps, an evolutionary link between reptiles and birds, which if true, would make "the working out of its embryology a matter of the greatest possible importance."[1] Wilson based his exciting hypothesis on an 1860 theory of German biologist-philosopher Ernst Haeckel, which proposed that vertebrate embryos reveal all prior stages of the organism's evolutionary history; this idea was probably the source of one we learned in school, that the human fetus progresses in the womb through successive stages of fish, reptile, and mammal.[2] A fresh embryo, Wilson believed, might clarify such questions as how bird feathers evolved from the scales of reptile ancestors. Indeed, one infers from his letter and journals that his unfinished inquiry on *A. forsteri* was the main cause of his return into the ice.

On January 19, 1911, the *Terra Nova* expedition arrived off Cape Crozier, where to Wilson's disappointment, rough seas prevented the establishment of the base close to the site of the dispersed colony. On the drift ice, he would spot an emperor chick in its first molt, its body still covered with gray down but its wings already feathered like an adult—the first chick observed in this stage of the life cycle—but in order to test his theory of the emperor's phylogeny and complete his monograph, he knew he must return to Crozier in the dark of winter.

Having estimated that the emperors must lay their eggs in late June or early July, "Bill" Wilson departed for Cape Crozier on June 26, 1911, accompanied by ship's officer Henry Bowers (called "Birdie" in celebration of his beakish nose), a small wiry Scotsman whose cheerful spirit, resourcefulness, and hardihood were to win him a last-minute

place in the group of five men chosen by Scott later that year for the final leg of the journey to the Pole. Wilson's other companion was a young "subscribing volunteer"—in effect, a paying guest on the expedition—named Apsley George Benet Cherry-Garrard. "Cherry" and "Birdie" had been picked not only as skilled sledgers but also as the two men he liked most, Wilson confided in a letter to his wife. "We want the scientific work to make bagging the Pole merely an item in the results," he added, an indication of his true interest in Scott's expedition. In the name of science, the doomed polar party would collect more than 30 pounds of geological specimens during the grueling return, clinging even in their desperate straits to the rather common *Glossopteris* fossils found with their bodies.

Setting off east around Ross Island over the frozen sea, the three hauled sledges over dangerous crevassed ice in bitter wind and biting cold down to −54°C, and perpetual darkness relieved only by fleeting moonlight, a dim midday twilight, and the wild glowing canopies of the aurora australis. As early as June 30, Cherry-Garrard doubted they would make it. "It was difficult not to howl," such was his misery, Cherry noted on July 2, the sixth day out; he was terrified and full of dread, marveling at the calm of his companions. Bill Wilson was "always patient, self-possessed, unruffled … the only man on Earth who could have led this journey." Birdie was cheerful and indomitable, with "few doubts and no fears. He made life look simple. Perhaps it really is."[3]

Not until July 15, after 19 days, did the party reach the east slope of Mount Terror, sloping down toward Crozier's 800-foot cliffs. A "breeding place of wind and drift and darkness," as Cherry would describe it, desperate to turn back. "I have never heard or felt or seen a wind like this. I wondered why it did not carry away the Earth."[4] Enduring unrelenting storm and horrific crises (their tent, blown away like a skua feather, was improbably recovered), the three men at last gazed down upon the rookery from the cliff above. "After indescribable effort and hardship, we were witnessing a marvel of the natural world."[5] Wilson and Bowers made the perilous descent, leaving Cherry behind to haul them back.

Due to savage conditions, this first visit to the rookery would be their last. The only three human beings (there have not been many since) who had ever viewed the emperor penguin brooding its lone egg in the polar winter had needed supreme perseverance and a near miracle to escape with their lives. Despite constant dread, Cherry had stood up to the test. "We kept our tempers, even with God," he wrote when the ordeal was over.[6]

Of the five eggs painfully collected, two were smashed by Cherry, who had lost his frozen eyeglasses and, near blind in the winter dark, was forever falling. Utterly defeated, low on supplies, the three set out on an interminable return, arriving at base camp ravaged and exhausted. Scott himself would declare that their winter journey to Cape Crozier was "the hardest … that has ever been made."

The three were scarcely rested and recovered when they set off with Scott for the south, establishing supply depots in support of the expedition to the Pole. Before departing, Wilson had written to the Royal Geographical Society, reporting the scientific progress of the expedition, and typically dismissing his own contribution in a single sentence: "My own effort in mid-winter to get to the Emperor Penguins at a time when their eggs would provide embryos fit for cutting [preparing slides for microscopic examination] turned out to be exceedingly difficult, but we succeeded in getting three different stages back which, I think, will prove to be of some interest." To this, he added (perhaps because the redoubtable Birdie Bowers was still expressing enthusiasm), "We shall make the rookery another visit next Spring."[7] Instead, Wilson and Bowers joined Scott, Captain Lawrence Oates, and an enlisted man, Edgar "Taff" Evans, on the final leg of the journey to the Pole.

Returning to England in 1913, Cherry-Garrard would deliver the three precious eggs to the British Museum (Natural History), where they were accepted so perfunctorily that he felt obliged to insist on a receipt—as if "it is an honour conferred upon the collector that his results should be accepted," he wrote tartly to the museum some years later, still rankling that the Cape Crozier ordeal, made worse by the tragic deaths of Wilson and Bowers on their return from the Pole a few months later, should have been repaid with such dull bureaucratic indifference. His friends the George Bernard Shaws (who urged Cherry to compose the memoir that would become *The Worst Journey in the World*) would assist in the caustic exchange with the museum provoked by Cherry's annoyed account of the slighted eggs.[8]

In 1914, the wandering eggs had been sectioned and examined by a specialist, Dr. Richard Assheton of Cambridge University, who unfortunately died in the next year with his report unfinished. Another expert, Dr. Professor Cossar Ewart of Edinburgh University, who submitted the "brief, preliminary report"[9] used in *The Worst Journey,* would venture that further study of these embryos might clarify the evolutionary relationship between scales and feathers, but unfortunately the task was still unfinished when he, too, died in 1933. By the time Assheton's sections were thoroughly examined by a third specialist, C. W. Parsons, more recent embryo collections had displaced them. In any case, Dr. Parsons concluded that in this stage of their development, Wilson's embryos "could not shed any new light on the problem of the ancestry of birds."[10] Since then, further studies have determined that penguins, far from being primitive, as Wilson thought, are specialized modern descendants of the flying birds. The worst journey in the world had been in vain.

At the time of *The Worst Journey*'s publication in 1922, the Antarctic coast, excepting the Ross Sea, was still unmapped except at a few points, and the interior remained all but unknown; nearly a half century would pass before Cape Crozier would be visited again. In 1957, snow tractors and aircraft facilitated the first overland expedition to arrive at the South Pole since Robert Falcon Scott in 1911. Sir Vivian Fuchs and Sir Edmund Hillary were its leaders, and Fuchs took time to motor out by tractor to Cape Crozier, where he located the stone ring of the Worst Journey igloo and confirmed the ongoing presence of the colony. The emperors, which may have been in residence under the cape for ten millennia before man put in his first appearance and may abide for thousands of years more unless drifting icebergs destroy the site or human activities melt it out from under them.

IN THE DAYS BEFORE icebreaker travel, a Ross Sea journey (other than tour flights to McMurdo and the South Pole station) was all but impossible to arrange. But by 2001, Victor Emanuel had organized a group of birders eager to be part of an emperor safari, and I signed on at once.

Just why, only three years after our first trip, with much work undone at home, I wished to make a far longer voyage to the ice was an intricate question. "To see the emperor penguin" was not good enough. I might mutter uncomfortably that Antarctica is monumental, an astonishment. Perhaps (if pressed) I might declare that its excruciating purity and vast healing silence ring with creation, ancient and yet new and fresh beyond imagining. More than any region left on Earth, I plead, Antarctica is immaculate, inviolable, a white fastness of pristine air and ice and virgin glacier at the farthest end of Earth, where frigid seas abound in marine creatures in a diversity still marvelously intact—all true, all true. Yet there is something else.

"Why do men who have returned [from the Antarctic] always wish to go back to that hard and simple life?" In a chapter on the psychology of Antarctic questers, which he later deleted from his book, Cherry-Garrard probed for this intricate truth. "I believe it to be this," he wrote. "A man on such an expedition lives so close to nature, in whom he realizes a giant force which is visibly, before his eyes, carving out the world."[11]

That sense of a "giant force" is surely part of it. Edward Wilson told his journal, "These days are with one for all time—they are never to be forgotten, and they are to be found nowhere else but at the poles."[12] In the terse opinion of Antarctica held by their *Terra Nova* shipmate, geologist Griffith Taylor, "There if anywhere is life worthwhile." Since we never learn why Wilson's polar days can be experienced nowhere else, nor what Taylor might mean by a "worthwhile" life—far less why its fulfillment is not possible outside of Antarctica— such generalities offer little insight that might help unlock the secret of what Ernest Shackleton would call the "longing for the Ice." A longing it most certainly is, but a longing for what?

"We had pierced the veneer of outside things"—Shackleton again. "We had seen God in his splendour, heard the text that nature renders. We had reached the naked soul of man." Such was expected in that era: all Glory to God, Our Redeemer, Creator. But the high-flown hyperbole of Antarctica's heroic age, resounding with invocations of creation, is no longer available to us poor moderns, no matter how awestruck one might feel—a pity, since the grandeur of Antarctica demands no less in the way of grandiloquence and grandiosity.

"The ancient and indifferent ice gives up its secrets slowly," someone else has said. At its glacial pace, the ice eventually relinquishes its mystery, whatever that might be. It clearly remained beyond articulation even by men who knew the ice firsthand under hard conditions.

Thus I struggle to find words for such wordless feeling: What draws me eludes me to the same degree, and seeking to understand rather than simply apprehend it may be just the problem.

IT EXCITES ME THAT our expedition will depart from Tasmania. Off the Antarctic Peninsula and its archipelagos three years before I was awed by the engulfing stillness of ice mountains, which in other ages had been southerly extensions of South America, the spine of the land bridge that connected Tierra del Fuego with Gondwana. Before the Andes were shifted eastward in the movements of tectonic plates, leaving the lowlands in between to be submerged by the circumpolar current that our ship had traversed on the return voyage to Cape Horn, the marsupials and monotremes, two early mammalian orders from the time of dinosaurs,[13] came sniffing across that land bridge, expanding their range into what became Antarctica, and leaving behind in the Americas the opossums, the last New World representatives of the ancient clan of the koala, bandicoot, and kangaroo.

No modern mammals carry and suckle their young in external pouches as marsupials do, nor lay leathery reptilelike eggs like the strange monotremes. Fossil evidence of monotremes from Patagonia and marsupials from the Peninsula has established that these immigrants were present in Antarctic Gondwana at least as early as 60 million years ago. Their descendants would spread west across Gondwana when it was still tropical to temperate in climate only to be borne back north when the Australian landmass, with New Guinea, broke away and withdrew from the Pole, leaving relatives to be extinguished by the growing cold.[14]

Thus, among the 17 to 26 mammalian orders (according to one's taxonomist), these groups became the only mammals native to Australia and Tasmania, and no others would invade their world for the next 20 million years. In the absence of competition, the marsupials (but not the monotremes) radiated into a wide range of ecological niches exploited elsewhere by more recent creatures: large and small carnivores, browsers and grazers, insectivores and nectar feeders, fast runners, hoppers, burrowers, climbers, gliders. Oddly, there are no flying marsupials. The expectation by ecologists that some sort of "marsupial bat" might be found to fill that niche was finally abandoned.

Eventually, Australia's continental shelf collided with the Asian shelf, permitting bats to immigrate from Indonesia. Rodents came later, probably on floating vegetation, but not until about 40,000 years ago did man turn up with his attendant dog. The feral dog known as the dingo is comparatively recent; it appeared only 7,000 to 8,000 years ago, introduced by a people probably related to those ancestral Maori who would settle New Zealand.

Ten millennia ago, as the seas rose in the wake of the last Ice Age, Tasmania became separated from mainland Australia. As the southernmost region of the continent, it represents the last region of the Australian Plateau to be formerly connected to Antarctica. Being remote and relatively unpopulated, the island retains most of its endemic marsupials and both of the egg-laying monotremes, the duck-billed platypus and the spiny echidna or "Australian porcupine."

In November 2001, a small advance group of field leaders and expedition members flew from California to Sydney, Australia, then south over the Bass Strait to Hobart, Tasmania, from where we would sail to Macquarie Island and the Ross Sea a few days later. Meanwhile our party would explore Tasmania under the expert guidance of Australian ornithologist Dion Hobcroft, who managed to show us all 13 of Tasmania's colorful endemic birds—those species, that is, that are not to be found anywhere else.

Since Tasmania and Tierra del Fuego, more than five thousand miles apart at the farthest points of the vast southern Pacific, were formerly connected by Gondwana, they might be visualized as northern points of that great landmass that at one time cupped the Southern Hemisphere. The fossil record has established kinships with Australia in the ancient flora of South America and Antarctica, including evidence that the southern beech (Nothofagus) forests that characterize both regions to this day and also dominated Antarctica for many million years. In Tasmania's Cradle Mountain and on Mount Wellington behind Hobart, we inspected an endemic beech closely related to a *Nothofagus* in those forests in Tierra del Fuego where, three years ago, we looked for the black Magellanic woodpecker, thought to be the closest relative of the majestic ivory-bill that is now all but extinct in North America.

As the last corner of Australia reached by man, Tasmania has preserved a greater variety and density of primitive mammals than the mainland, but even here, at least one marsupial has been extinguished since *Homo sapiens* first intruded on its peace and quiet. Last seen alive in the 1930s was a coyote-size carnivore called the thylacine, popularly known from the black flank stripes on its tawny body as the "Tasmanian tiger;" some believe it may still survive in the wilder mountains. At the Tasmania Museum on Macquarie Street, where we were shown two thylacine skins, there was talk of extracting its DNA and re-creating a cloned replica of that gaunt, unprepossessing animal. Because no such precise replication occurs in nature, there is something unnatural and "dead" about a clone, as there is about almost anything identified as a mere copy. Though I kept my opinion to myself, it seemed to me that the considerable cost of this experiment might be better applied to preserving habitat for Tasmania's endangered species.

Almost everywhere, we came across marsupials—kangaroos and wallabies, tree possums, wombats, pademelons, and the swift little creature known as the bandicoot. In the woods of Mole Creek, a young conservationist named Androo Kelly showed us a captive group of the threatened marsupial known as the Tasmanian Devil, a black fox-size carnivore that he is breeding in captivity as part of an effort to restore its wild populations. Elsewhere, we found both monotremes, the spiny echidna (at Cradle Mountain in northwestern Tasmania and elsewhere) and a pair of duck-billed platypuses, which popped to the surface like rubber toys as they fed at dusk under a bridge across the Mersey River.

To travel from Tierra del Fuego to this sanctuary of old Gondwanan mammals in Tasmania is to come full circle, and being an old mammal myself, I apprehend it as one way of going home.

What end is there to the pure wind,
circling the Earth?
—Blue Cliff Record

All the universe is one bright pearl.
What need is there to understand it?
—Zen Master Dogen

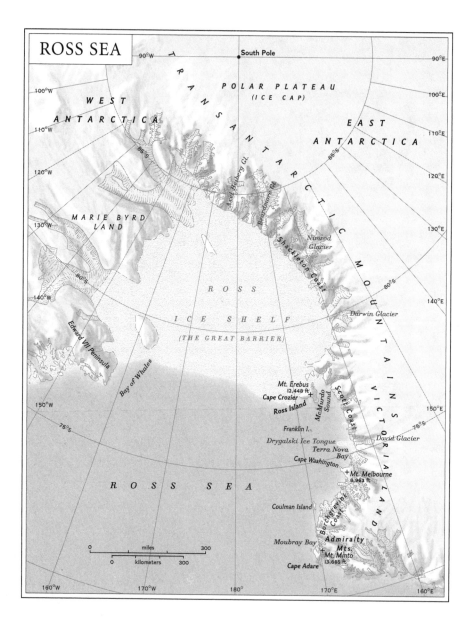

ROSS SEA

South Pole

POLAR PLATEAU
(ICE CAP)

WEST
ANTARCTICA

EAST
ANTARCTICA

T R A N S A N T A R C T I C

M O U N T A I N S

MARIE BYRD
LAND

Ice Melberg Gl.

Beardmore Gl.

Nimrod
Glacier

Shackleton Coast

R O S S

I C E   S H E L F

(THE GREAT BARRIER)

Darwin Glacier

Edward VII Peninsula

Bay of Whales

Mt. Erebus
12,448 ft
Cape Crozier
Ross Island

Franklin I.

McMurdo Sound

Scott Coast

V I C T O R I A   L A N D

David Glacier

Drygalski Ice Tongue
Terra Nova
Bay
Cape Washington

Mt. Melbourne
8,963 ft

Coulman Island

Borchgrevink Coast

R O S S   S E A

Moubray Bay

Admiralty
Mts.
Mt. Minto
13,665 ft

Cape Adare

miles   300

kilometers   300

part three

THE ICE REFLECTED
ON THE CLOUDS

LEAVING TASMANIA

From her black hull, the mustard superstructure of the polar ice-breaker *Kapitan Khlebnikov* rises deck upon deck like a Third World cell block or high-rise economy motel, ruling the pretty waterfront of Hobart, and filling the heart of the prospective passenger with misgiving. This top-heavy hulk of shallow draft, designed for frozen river deltas and shipping channels along the Arctic coast, must voyage nearly 2,000 miles across the roughest ocean in the world, rolling like a Russian doll the entire way, before reaching the edges of the great ice that guards Antarctica. Penetrating the white wastes north of the Ross Sea, she will cross the Antarctic Circle and bash south at least as far as Terra Nova Bay and the Drygalski Ice Tongue, some 600 miles beyond the southernmost point on our 1998 voyage to the Antarctic Peninsula.

"Our job is to deliver passengers to places where no other ship can go," Captain Viktor Vasil'yev says dutifully at dinner this first evening. A small man with cropped hair and gold-capped teeth, Captain Viktor is very experienced with "the ice," having served as 3rd and 2nd mate on other icebreakers before being made master of the *Khlebnikov* when she was commissioned in 1981; he served for a decade in Siberia, opening channels from her home port at

Vladivostok north to Magadan, the Kamchatka Peninsula, and the Bering Strait, then 2,000 miles west along the Arctic coast to the mouth of the Lena River.

The *K*'s overall length is 129.10 meters (423.5 feet), and she draws 8.5 meters (28 feet). Weighing 12,000 tons, with a hull plate of 45-millimeter steel backed by heavy steel frames spaced closely near the waterline, she is powered by six diesel-electric engines that generate 24,000 hp. In addition to her crew of 54 (she had 90 as an icebreaker, says Captain Viktor), she carries approximately that same number of passengers, most of them clients of Victor Emanuel Nature Tours, a wildlife safari company out of Austin, Texas, but also a covey of keen British birders and a shy small cluster of nonbirders from Taiwan.[1]

Werner Stambach, the able young German whose Quark Expeditions travel company has leased her from the Far Eastern Shipping Company in Vladivostok, calls the *Khlebnikov* "a fully classed polar icebreaker," much more powerful than conventional ships and far better equipped to deal with heavy pack ice: In fact, the *K* was the first passenger ship to circumnavigate Antarctica. Heading south a month ahead of the summer travel season, before the breakup of the icepack is well under way, she will sight no other vessel in Antarctic waters. The purpose of our early start is to witness a spectacle that few ornithologists have been fortunate enough to see, the emperor penguin breeding colonies that have been discovered at a few remote (and not always accessible) locations that the ship must reach before the colonies disperse.

Werner Stambach, who has made 40 or more voyages to remote destinations in the Arctic and Antarctic, is a lean, tanned, balding German of about 40; his wife, Olga, is a pretty young Russian from Murmansk on the Arctic Ocean. Whether on rolling deck or at the podium, Werner's preferred stance is legs wide apart and arms akimbo, as if to project the bold swashbuckling spirit of Quark Expeditions, Inc. Werner is confident that the *K* can approach at least two of the three emperor colonies along the Ross Sea's western coast.

"Well, at least one," cautions his sensible assistant, the American naturalist and educator Susan Adie.

Since our 1998 voyage, the Antarctic Peninsula has become a regular cruise ship destination for more than 12,000 tourists every year. Almost all of these ships set out from South America or the Falklands, a far shorter journey with less risk of the boisterous weather that may scare travelers away from the Southern Ocean. Victor is proud that ours is the first voyage by an American bird-tour company to the remote colonies of the emperor penguin.

AT FIVE P.M. ON NOVEMBER 25, on a lovely late spring evening, the *K* descends the Derwent River, whose lower reach, between rolling high green hills, serves Hobart as a natural deepwater harbor. The lighthouse on a small island off the river mouth marks the traditional spot where in 1642, the Dutch navigator Abel Tasman, rounding this coast to determine if south Australia was attached to the mysterious Terra Incognita Australis, became the first European to set foot on what he called Van Diemen's Land, after the governor of the Dutch East Indies. We scan in vain for the small blue penguin once common on these coasts, which in recent years have become so developed that the birds sometimes make nesting burrows under seaside bungalows and are often seen at large in the night streets.

The *K* scatters an assemblage of short-tailed shearwaters, long-winged gray-brown seabirds that migrate to the North Pacific in the austral winter and appear off the coast of California before returning here to breed on offshore islands. The unfledged young, called "muttonbirds," formerly harvested for oil and meat by Aborigines and early sealers, were "moonbirds" to the tribal people, so vital to the cycle of natural foods that a clan using bark craft to travel yearly to the rookery islands called itself the Moonbird People.[2] Shearwaters share with albatrosses a long aerodynamic wing for ocean sailing, and watching them here within sight of land, I wondered if that wing shape and wind-carving glide might not have influenced the evolution of the boomerang.

As if to replace the harbor pilot, who hops down into his launch, swift hourglass dolphins, white and black, escort the ship as she emerges from the sheltering green hills into the Tasman Sea. Shards of platinum marble the dark clouds of a departing weather front to westward. In summer in these latitudes, sunset comes late, and it will come ever later as we journey south. Dim night is falling about 8:45 p.m. as Tasmania sinks behind the waves and the *K* sets her course for Macquarie Island, 930 miles to the southeast, her only landfall before reaching the ice.

On icebreakers, the bridge and helm are elevated as high as possible, the better to scan for open leads in the ice ahead. My cabin is located on the outside starboard corner of Deck 8, just below the bridge, where during the night, as the roll increased, I slid up and down my bunk like a short corpse in a long coffin.

SAILING FROM HOBART brings to mind the British explorer James Clark Ross, who arrived in Tasmania by way of the Crozet Islands (where the smelly sealers were "more like Esquimaux than civilized beings") and the wind-battered Kerguélens. Aboard the *Erebus* and her sister ship the *Terror,* Ross's British National Expedition to Antarctica sailed down the Derwent on November 12, 1840, escorted on the *Erebus* by Tasmania's Governor Sir John Franklin, a former and future explorer in the Canadian Arctic who would utterly vanish with these same Admiralty ships a few years later while leading an expedition to open a Northwest Passage route to the Pacific.

The Royal Navy's Captain Ross was already a veteran of four Arctic voyages, on one of which, in 1831, he had located the north magnetic pole. Intent on claiming the same prize in the south, he was chagrined that the French explorer Jules-Sébastien-César Dumont d'Urville had preceded him to his chosen Antarctic region of Australia in the previous year. ("All the time that doubts were possible," Dumont d'Urville wrote in the afternoon of January 19, 1839, "I had not wanted to give my name to this discovery, but when our boats returned I gave it the name Adélie Land." Though he mentions neither his wife Adéle Dorothée nor the penguins, he gave her name to these ice birds, too, while he was at it.[3]) In the same summer, Lt. Charles Wilkes, a skilled navigator and mapmaker in command of three American vessels on a voyage of exploration to Antarctica and the Pacific (1838-42), asserted that the Frenchman had arrived "a few days after the same coast was seen by ships of my squadron." Unfortunately, the American's claim was not supported by his navigational bearings, which Ross, among others, rejected indeed, Wilkes was accused at an 1842 court-martial of "deliberate and wilfull falsehood." Nonetheless, Wilkes's vessels explored farther along the icebound mainland coast than anyone before him,[4] and he was also the first navigator to state correctly and without equivocation that "we have discovered not a range of detached islands but a vast Antarctic continent," a claim that Ross's voyage would confirm. Though chastised for his "harsh, overbearing, and insulting" abuse and discipline of his officers and men, Wilkes was eventually awarded the rank of rear admiral and a Founder's Medal from the Royal Geographical Society. Dumont d'Urville, too, would be made an admiral, though his foray south of the Antarctic Circle lasted but a month, round trip from Hobart.

Charles Wilkes had been "friendly and honorable enough" to supply Ross with the charts of his own voyage. Together with the journals of the British sealer John Balleny, these charts persuaded Ross that his precursors had been working too far west, where

Balleny had been blocked by heavy pack ice near the 172nd meridian of longitude. Being anxious to avoid known territory, Ross sailed eastward to the Aucklands, south of New Zealand, before heading south on the 170th meridian by way of Campbell Island, which Balleny thought might lead to an opening through the pack ice. On January 11, 1841, Ross sighted Cape Adare, the northwest portal of an enormous unknown sea that, as he would discover in the weeks that followed, extended southward another 500 miles toward the Pole.

By Ross's time, the icebound continent—or its white ice cliffs or its mists—had been tentatively sighted at several points; Thaddeus von Bellingshausen seems to have come within 20 miles of it even before his discovery in 1819 of what would be recognized as "the first certain land in the Antarctic ... Alexander Land ... nearly due south of Cape Horn."[5] Until Bellingshausen, Weddell, and Ross discovered the seas named for them, it had been assumed that the Terra Incognita was an ice-mantled circular landmass with the South Pole at its center and an outer boundary roughly delineated by the Antarctic Circle.

Though *Erebus* and *Terror,* like Cook's *Resolution* and *Adventure,* were beamy, rugged work vessels from northern England, it seems extraordinary that such craft penetrated so far south under sail, especially when one considers that the *Erebus* was a 392-ton wooden ship, less than one-thirtieth the weight of our steel icebreaker.

In the half century after Ross (1839-43), Antarctic exploration was limited to one British expedition of 1872-76 led by Captain George Nares. His *Challenger* was the first vessel to cross the Circle under steam, and her circumpolar voyage gathered scientific data at regular intervals. The rocks released by melting icebergs, retrieved from the polar ocean bottom, would bear out Wilkes's conviction that Antarctica was a true continent, not an archipelago of glaciated islands—a matter of lingering doubt among Ross's detractors even after his exploration of the Ross Sea.

SOUTHERN OCEAN

By dawn, the *K* has entered the realm of silent ocean birds—the great royal albatross and seven petrel species.[6] Her position at noon is 46.34° south latitude. Though deep into the Roaring Forties, we enjoy a day of light westerly winds and a mild temperature of 55°F. White-sided dolphins slash through fish shoals off the starboard quarter, and somebody reports a distant whale. Most of the sighting is done from bow and stern as well as the bridge roof, but some of the birders take shelter inside on the bridge, where big windows that overlook the fore-deck and the bow extend across the whole width of the ship.

At 6:30 a.m., a wandering albatross is sailing across the wake, and an hour later, there are four, attended by another *Diomedea* called the shy albatross. The huge wandering and royal albatrosses are readily distinguished from the smaller "mollymawks"—the black-browed, shy, gray-headed, and light-mantled—all of which are frequently observed in the temperate seas north of Macquarie.

Southern Ocean birds (all but the skua), spanning the meridians on the strong winds, can drink seawater and excrete the salt—a necessary adaptation, as mentioned earlier, in pelagic birds whose nonbreeding subadults may spend years at sea out of sight of land. It is the transience of gale birds, their seeming frailty in the toils of wind and sea, that stirs me most. To see a lone petrel arc across some desolate reach of ocean, as fleeting as the spray blown from the wave crests, is to risk unnameable intuitions of mortal solitude and transience, one's own swift passage toward the void.

The oceanic petrels, especially the small species known as whalebirds or prions and the storm-petrels, which are smaller still, are often difficult to distinguish; the larger species of the genus *Pterodroma*, dark birds that maintain a distance, are not much easier. The procellarids that most passengers learn quickly are the white-spotted, chocolate pintado or Cape petrel, and, farther south, the gull-like silver or southern fulmar. Both of these species, like the hulking giant-petrels, seem drawn to ships, passing up and down on the ship's air currents and coursing the white wake.

Despite differences in feeding habits—the broad-billed prion sieves its plankton, for example, whereas the Antarctic prion picks it from the surface—the blue-gray prions are generally so similar that the validity of several species is still disputed. At present, from three to six "good" species are recognized, but seen in rough weather through wind-teared eyes and binoculars salt-misted by spray, most whalebirds are noted down as "prion species" unless they pass close alongside or beneath the bow.

The British birders are led by an affable expert on southern pelagic birds named Tony Pym—no known relation to that Arthur Gordon Pym sent to Terra Australis by Edgar Allan Poe in 1845— whose identifications are mostly agreed with by Victor Emanuel and Greg Lasley, the professional ornithologists in our group. (The Batemans and I, although knowledgeable, are professionals in other fields, with limited experience in the Southern Ocean.) In addition to the ornithologists, excellent staff lecturers[7] provided by the ship introduce wildlife, sea and ice, and other vagaries of Antarctic life to those not seasick in their bunks or otherwise indifferent to these matters.

MACQUARIE ISLAND

Toward daybreak, at 54° 37 minutes south latitude the ship makes landfall at Macquarie Island. About 5:45 a.m., as I awake, white-headed petrels pass my rolling porthole. I reach the deck in time to celebrate the squads of gold-crested royal penguins that burst through the bow wave like flying fish to escape the hull, shooting, tumbling, somersaulting, pink feet flying.

The solitary point of land between Tasmania and the Ross Sea, Macquarie is one of eight storm-swept sub-Antarctic islands along the cold-water boundary called the Antarctic Convergence or Polar Front, which roughly delineates the northern limit of the Antarctic ice pack in the southern winters.[8] Though Macquarie lies north of the front, the fairy prions have already been replaced by Antarctic prions.

As a breeding concentration of southern seabirds and marine mammals, Macquarie ranks with South Georgia as a destination. Low-lying and unglaciated, the island is eroded not by ice but by violent ocean weather, with almost incessant strong westerly winds, battering waves, and unrelenting rains.

Unlike most of the Southern Ocean's remote islands, which developed as undersea volcanoes, Macquarie is an emergent ridge of a great drowned mountain system surrounded by trenches up to three miles deep; it is the only island on Earth composed entirely of ancient crust and rock from the Earth's mantle. Thus the exposed crust on the north part of the island, forced upward from a region at least a mile beneath the mile-deep ocean floor, is invaluable for study of the Earth's geologic processes such as plate tectonics and continental drift. Though its rock is thought to be 27 million years old, Macquarie is relatively recent as an island, breaking the ocean surface within the last half million years. It is still rising, with chronic earth tremors and landslips, made worse by heavy rains.[9]

Coming in from the northwest toward the north cape, the ship turns south along the windward coast. Because the island points north and south, across the path of prevailing winds and currents, cliffs and ravines disappear into the thick sea mists on the ridge, and a heavy surf crashes on the black volcanic boulders along shore. The island suffers a mean annual temperature of 41°F and an average of 300 days and 34 inches of rain. "The most wretched place of involuntary and slavish *exilium* that can possibly be conceived; nothing could warrant any civilized creature living in such a spot," a Captain

Douglass reported in 1822; he did not tarry. Lieutenant Charles Wilkes, exploring southward in 1839, paused at Macquarie to harvest seals and penguins for the larder, taking time to note that the island "affords no inducement for a visit."[10]

Deemed unfit even for a penal colony by a government nearly a thousand miles off to the north, the island was wide open to commercial exploitation. Within five months of its discovery in 1810 by Australian sealer Frederick Hasselborough,[11] four sealing gangs had slaughtered some 17,000 fur seals on their breeding grounds; within a few years, more than 19 out of 20 of an estimated 200,000 "upland seals" had been destroyed.[12] Soon thereafter, the few survivors vanished, not to reappear until after World War II. The first pup in 130 years was recorded in 1965, but seal numbers remained small until the 1980s, when a viable population became established for the first time in well over a century, in stirring evidence of the resilience and tenacity of most wild creatures.

As in South Georgia, the fur seal slaughter shifted quickly to the huge elephant seals, which were rendered for their oil. By 1880, a population of 110,000 elephants had been reduced to less than a thousand, at which time a penguin harvest was begun. The birds were herded into pens and clubbed, then heaped into steam boilers called "digesters." Joseph Burton, who worked at Macquarie as a penguin "collector" for three years near the turn of the century, wrote that "the royals are good for the amount of oil they yield when boiled down [about 1 pint apiece].... As many as 2000 birds can be put through the digesters in a day, equal to fourteen casks of oil, each about forty gallons."[13] Burton noted that while "the island is dreadfully dreary to the ordinary observer, to the naturalist it is full of fascinating interest."

Dr. Edward Wilson, bound for Antarctica on the *Discovery* in 1901, collected bird specimens on Macquarie for three hours on November 22, feeling fortunate to see "four or five rails of a kind [of] which no museum in Europe possesses a specimen, except Rothschild and he only one." Wilson was much amused when his friend "Shackle," gathering penguin eggs for food, saw one fall from a king penguin that Wilson had lifted by the neck. Not realizing that the egg had been nestled on its upturned feet, Shackleton assured the others in the shore party that they had only to throttle the bird as Wilson was doing to make it lay.

On his return to England from Antarctica in 1904, Wilson spoke out in defense of Macquarie's penguins. "The hunting of King Penguins into red-hot cauldrons for their oil will shock their graces, I think, but it is done at Macquarie Island."[14]

In 1911, Australian geologist and redoubtable Antarctic explorer Douglas Mawson would lead a campaign to spare Macquarie's fauna, calling this island "one of the wonder spots of the world ... the great focus of the seal and bird life in the Australasian and Antarctic regions." The penguin slaughter was finally ended in 1919, by which time the island's endemic rail and parakeet were extinct, the victims of man's rats and cats and also of the weka or "Maori hen," introduced from New Zealand as a source of food. Macquarie's fauna was so diminished by man's interference that several species such as the common diving-petrel, almost identical to the Georgian diving-petrel we had seen at South Georgia halfway around the world, confined their nesting to offshore rocks that the introduced predators could not reach. The weka and the feral cats, at least, are now almost eradicated, and prions are nesting here again, and the blue petrel, which has raised its first known young in 130 years.

EVEN NOW, IN EARLY SUMMER, Macquarie can draw snow squalls, and its winds are constant. Yesterday's easterly wind is shifting to the north-northwest as the ship rounds Hurd Point—the southern cape—where seas explode against high dark pinnacles of rock. Heading north again under the lee shore off Lusitania Bay, she slows and idles so that her passengers may inspect an immense rookery containing an estimated 850,000 royal penguins. Like an upside-down fan, the bright white breasts ascend a gravel slope to the mouth of a ravine that parts a green plateau, which climbs in turn to a ridge perhaps 1,200 feet high. On these plateaus are several lakes, including one of more than 100 acres, allegedly frequented by mallards introduced in the 19th century to Australia and New Zealand and thought to have wandered to Macquarie of their own accord.

The island, three miles at its widest, has no protected harbor, but in moderate weather, a few coves on the lee coast are accessible to our small craft. At shallow Buckles Bay near the north end, the island narrows to an isthmus, and here the ship anchors a quarter mile offshore, where advance parties of king penguins swim to greet us. Flipping and diving to make way for the black hull, they regroup and advance again, crossing the surface in noisy squadrons or shooting underwater in gold-greenish streams of bubbles clearly visible from the ship's decks. As a noon sun comes and goes, the flame-headed birds flash through the water, while from the shore come weird metallic wailings interspersed by the moans of seals.

Four Zodiacs are swung over the side and brought around to the lowered gangway, but the wind has risen to 25 to 30 knots, with gusts to 50, blowing across the sands of the low isthmus, and the heavy swells on the windward coast are rounding the north point, with a back swell into the bay. Despite skillful handling of the outboard boats, a surge of 10 to 15 feet at the gangway makes the transfer of the less fit a precarious business, and one elderly birder, Ida Girunas of Massachusetts, is plunged up to the neck in frigid water. Though Ida herself returned aboard with high spirits scarcely dampened, the sight of her misadventure would cause others to withdraw from the shore party, in hopes that the wind might moderate during the night.

Administered by Tasmanian National Parks, Macquarie was made a world Biosphere Reserve and a World Heritage site in 1977, and the Australian government enforces strict environmental restraints on any visitors. Before boarding the small boats, we step into a tub of chemicals so that our boots will not contaminate the island ecosystem with exotic germs or seeds or insects, and ashore one is monitored by designated rangers from the research station north of the landing, assigned to protect the island life from heedless behavior.

Visitors are divided into groups according to energy and inclination. I am leader of the "long walk" group—those who wish to stretch their legs while visiting the bird and sea mammal colonies across the isthmus on the windward shore. In the care of two young lady rangers, Georgie and Sandy, we set off at once to a low rise known optimistically as the Lookout, from where we enjoy the light-mantled sooty albatrosses and nesting skuas that sail up and down the grassy hillsides on the air currents. Even these strong fliers, obliged to take shelter from the wind, remain below the ridgeline of steep hills scarred brown by landslips of unstable soil. Though Macquarie's climate is too cold for shrubs and trees, it supports a heavy growth of megaherbs such as Macquarie cabbage *Stilbocarpa polaris*, used as a source of vitamin C to prevent scurvy, and the sage-green cushion plant *Pleurophyllum hookeri*, named for Ross's inspired botanist Joseph Hooker.

Descending, we cross the isthmus to the black rock and thunder of the windward shore, where the wind spins us half around and lashes our faces with stinging sand. The upper beach is laden with brown giant kelp and elephant seal bulls with their harems. The groaning animals lift their heads and blink strange glazed eyes like black moons that are so eerily reminiscent of the blank black eyes of the white sharks—"white pointers," as Australians call them—that bashed against our lowered cage in 1969, off seal rocks south of Australia's southern coast.[15]

Seal bones, skulls, and leather carcasses are tangled in the twisted beds of storm wrack kelp, for the huge seals, up to 14 feet long, use this beach to fight and die as well as breed, and mating takes place in the midst of the birthing and dying. Most are engaged in the annual molting of old coats, with much rubbing up against the others to this end. Every bull is heavily scarred, and one is half-blinded by the socket of green pus where his left eye had been; he may be too weakened by his combat wounds to leave the beach.

A colossal bull drapes an avuncular flipper over a desperate little female not one tenth his weight, which may approach four tons. (Since genitalia and mammary glands are encased in fat, it might be difficult to sex these animals were it not for the great discrepancy in size found in harem species.) While she flops wildly, seeking to escape, he is trying to draw her toward his belly where his tool protrudes, he has already ravished her, to judge from her bloody hind end. One longs to dash forward and break it up—"Unhand her, brute!" Ordinarily the bull does not lie atop his mate but takes her sideways; even so, his elephantine throes may kill the young female or her last year's pup.

Giant-petrels, including a white one stained by carrion, are looting a putrified bull carcass, already reduced to a collapsed leather sac spilling near-slime. To drive off rivals, the hunched vulturish birds hop sideways on half-opened wings, ragged tails obscenely cocked; they shoot horrid heads through holes in the hide and emerge, heavy beaks dripping.

Farther on, small gentoo companies from a colony high on the slope plod up and down the little streambed, which serves them as a path down to the sea. The 5,000-odd pairs on Macquarie are the only breeding gentoos in the Indo-Pacific region of the Southern Ocean. Here they run a gantlet of king penguins, which chivvy the much smaller birds along. When the rain gives way to fleeting sun, the fire-throated kings reflect the wild lights of blue and turquoise surf. Crashing among black and ancient rocks, the rude waves swirl the glistening bronze tentacles of giant kelp.

Humpback Whale, Lemaire Channel, Antarctic Peninsula

Emperor Penguin Colony, Cape Roget

Bulbinella rossi, *Campbell Island*

King Penguins (and Robert Bateman sketching), Fortuna Bay, South Georgia

Icebreaker Kapitan Khlebnikov, *170th Meridian*

Emperor Penguin Colony, Cape Washington

Ice, Ross Sea

Royal Albatross, South Georgia Island

Hooker's Sea Lions, Macquarie Island

Gentoo Penguin, Hannah Point, Livingston Island

Elephant Seals, Hannah Point

ON THE WAY TO TEA and scones with the rangers and research personnel at the research station, we pass the rusting boilers used to extract subcutaneous fat from the slaughtered penguins; beyond the tryworks stand the huts of the Australia National Antarctic Research Expedition (ANARE).[16] We can scarcely walk against the burly wind, and the rain stings. "The weather here is universally fairly foul," sighs Rod Ledingham of the ship's staff, a husky bearded Scot with a wry wit who has been a geologist in western Australia and a dogsled driver; he once wintered inadvertently on the Antarctic Peninsula after his departing aircraft made a crash landing on take-off. A longtime official of ANARE, Rod was formerly director of this "Macca" Station.

I was leaving the mess hut when a pod of orca—three to seven animals, depending on the imaginations of those yelling—cruised past the landing, hunting along shore for seals and penguins; the big creatures had passed beneath the Zodiac operated by ANARE's Mick Davidson, a staffer on our voyage who was returning people to the ship. Hearing the yells, I ran for the landing but arrived too late—to my great regret, since I had yet to see "killer whales" in the Southern Ocean. "Killer whales" are not true whales, but large bottle-nosed dolphins, nor are they credited with killing human beings, despite scaring reports from Scott's expedition and many others.[17]

Before returning to the ship, we visited a rocky cove to observe a small colony of the notoriously ill-tempered rockhopper penguins. Some were engaged in hopping crossly up their rocks while others—hopping mad, no doubt—come bouncing down. Unlike most penguins, the rockhopper often jumps feetfirst into the sea—out of sheer perversity, I like to think. Due apparently to habitat disruption caused by climate change, the small, feisty rockhopper of the sub-Antarctic is in drastic decline all around the Southern Ocean.

BUCKLES BAY ON A BRIGHT morning of whitecaps and white birds: a black-browed albatross, a white giant-petrel, the white breasts of prions, flashing and chasing over cold blue water. The wind out of the north-northwest is hard and steady. My large squarish porthole high on the ship's superstructure frames the isthmus, the ANARE station, and the abrupt headland at the north end of the island where black rocks off the point disappear one by one under the surf as they march down the drowned mountainside into the abyss.

The ship weighs anchor and moves south to Sandy Bay, where the island's central ridge provides a lee. Royal and king penguins not otherwise engaged rush off the beaches to surround the ship, shooting about under the shining surface; we trace their path by the flash of gold and the sheath of silver bubbles. Ashore, staid committees of noble kings waddle forth to welcome us as we swing off the boat's bow into the shallows; they raise long, curved bills toward the heavens to squall their metallic cry while bumping aside the few pesky royals which run to join the ceremony.

North up the beach, a small colony of kings includes young of every size from egg dweller to "Oakum Boy"—a nickname for the bulky chicks still clad in dull brown down. (Since none of the Aussies or Tasies aboard ship seems to know the provenance of that name, I'm free to speculate that the brown fuzz reminded old-time seafarers of the frayed oakum caulking between timbers on the wooden decks.) The Macquarie kings, 100,000 pairs, remain at lower elevations, too heavy and dignified to attempt the high ascents made by uppity small penguins such as the royal.

Like the rockhopper, the royal is one of six *Eudyptes* or crested penguins, which include the similar macaroni of the Western Hemisphere and three rare localized species of New Zealand and its islands. Like most penguins (and many other water birds, and most shorebirds, too), the royal is dark above and white below, an evolutionary design that may serve to fragment its silhouette as a defense against undersea predators; also, the dark mantle absorbs heat. It has pink feet and a red-orange bill and a pink patch extending from the lower mandible toward the eye. However, its glory lies in its twin spikes of golden feathers, which flare back rakishly from each brow like the wings of Mercury's helmet, only to collapse behind the eye like a fallen hairpiece.

Though abundant here, the royal penguin breeds only on Macquarie Island, where an estimated 850,000 pairs are resident in half a hundred colonies that may climb hundreds of feet up the steep slopes. Like other *Eudyptes*, the royal usually lays two eggs, discarding the first after the appearance of the second, which is heavier and more auspicious on that account.[18]

The heart of royal penguin territory at Sandy Bay is on a pebble-lined bench high above the shore in the heavy tussock grass. Here a colony of 20,000 pairs extends over a rise and continues intermittently up the mountain to an outpost on the highest slope, where a landslip has laid the gravel bare of soil and vegetation. Why penguins would choose to trudge uphill, perhaps for hours, ascending the stones of a trickling brook toward a point hundreds of feet above sea level and well over a mile from the salt water seems a great mystery, since there is ample open territory at lower levels.[19]

In one small area, a hillside depression, some 2,000 royals tend their large eggs and a few early chicks, guarding the crowded pebble nests against the sharp-eyed skuas with incessant squawking, gobbling, and pecking threats toward surrounding neighbors. Both of the egg's parents may be present, pressing close to reinforce the pair bond against the stress of empty days when one mate is off at sea, and as they groom and preen each other, their crest-fallen gold plumes seem to spring to life.

According to Melissa Giese of the Australian Parks and Wildlife Service, the young biologist who is studying this colony, the last week of incubation and the first three weeks of chick-tending are performed by the male, which goes hungry for 40 days while the female is off foraging at sea, gathering food to pump into the hatchling; the distances royal penguins swim may exceed 200 miles, or 30 hour's travel in three days. Wide-ranging kings have been tracked almost as far as Campbell Island, New Zealand, 400 miles away, which we shall visit on the northward voyage from Antarctica.

In the warm hollow on the hillside, sheltered from the wind by sun-shined tussock, the penguin field is a hallucinating pattern of black, white, and gold, or so I see it in the ocean light and the wild racketing and ricocheting squall and moan of seabird companies.

Nearby, Birgit and Bob Bateman are happily recording the royal spectacle. Since becoming acquainted in 1998, we have traveled together to India and Texas, and Bob Bateman is finishing a series of fine paintings for our recent book on the 15 species of cranes around the world.[20] Another bond is a perverse fondness for this acrid guano smell, which we associate with remote coasts and sea cliffs and rock islands, and also with sea-bright days like this one, as rare on Macquarie as they were on South Georgia, for which all of us are very grateful. The world is shining—the penguin heads, the tussock grass, the gold-brown pelage of the loaflike giants slumbering along the shore, and perhaps especially the gleaming straps of bull kelp, reflecting sun as with each surge they writhe among the sea rocks, like the arms of a famished octopus emerged from the dark abysses around the island.

South along the shore is a sheltered place among columns of odd basaltic rocks called "pillow boulders." Here another small colony of rockhoppers makes its home. On the shore cliffs are nesting blue-eyed shags, whose cobalt eye rings and the orange caruncles at the base of the bill are especially bright during the breeding season.[21] Stretched on the brown algae of a flat rock at the water's edge is an eared seal, a young male, dark brown, which Rod Ledingham identifies as an Antarctic fur seal—quite possibly the "upland seal" that was all but exterminated in the island's early history. Overhead, in a slow dreaming, wheel light-mantled albatrosses. One alights at its cliffside nest, well hidden from the figures in the boat that it sees craning upward from below.

ANTARCTIC OCEAN

A low-pressure front of heavy wind and rain is forecast for the region. The ship flees before it, for the ice is still heavy in the Ross Sea approaches that must be penetrated if we are to reach Terra Nova Bay and the redoubts of the emperor penguin before their colonies disperse into the ocean.

Clearing Point Hurd in early afternoon, the *K* moves out of the island's lee into the wind, as the steep-sided rock ridge in her wake— the lonely summit of unimaginable drowned mountains—subsides gradually into the sea. In austral light, long cresting waves have a wild silver sheen, all across the leagues of sea to the west horizon.

By mid-afternoon, the sinking island far astern is smothered by incoming mists, but in the south there is sun and a blue sky. Leaned against the bulkhead out of the wind, I am eased into near somnolence by the ship's roll, watching the birds gather from the distances to glide across the blue churning of the wake. Among them is one odd-looking albatross, smaller and more compact. Though I point it out to Victor, he is unable to identify it before it vanishes under the skyline, nor can we find it later in the books—it is lost forever. "Mystery birds" are frustrating and a bit humbling, too, though no doubt salutary in the development of birding character.

In the ocean deeps beneath the hull is a dark realm of plateaus and abysses created by the rupturing of the Earth's crust; over many thousands of square miles, the only points where ridges break the ocean surface are Macquarie Island and Campbell Island, 400 miles away to the northeast. From marine charts on the bridge, I roughly estimate the time when the ship will pass over the Macquarie Trench; that hour comes in mid-afternoon. The knowledge that an astonishing abyss lies three miles below our hull is stirring, though once again, I cannot imagine why this should be so. If discernible at all from such a depth, our tiny ship in silhouette against the sun can be no more than a black mote in the glimmer far above, as distant as the glint of an aircraft passing between clouds three miles above.

The lone sentinel island, the eastering seas, the infinite horizons all around the ocean sky: All is beautiful and wild and free—the beauty "that is inconceivable because it runs through all eternity," as one Antarctic chronicler described it.[22] Oddly, time draws to a stop, as in that moment at the crest of the flood, the lunar pause before the slow turn of the tide toward its ebb. Out of that suspended moment, like a held breath, rises the question of how and why this corpus with my attached name and history came to fetch up here in just this moment of a fleeting life, on a lone vessel in the farthest reaches of the Southern Ocean, bound for an ice-locked continent a thousand miles beyond that south horizon.

Some deeper quest, or so I think, must lie beneath this pilgrimage to behold the emperor penguin. In my case, the quest must have something to do with a lifelong need not to simplify my life—though I need that, too—but to "simplify my self," as noted earlier. Meanwhile, I am quite content with the material simplicity of shipboard life. Though scarcely hermetic, it offers a cocoon free of incoming mail, the clamor of the telephone, intrusive voices. In my spare small cabin with its bunk and desk, its big porthole like a window on the sea, my books, binoculars, warming whiskey, and rare solitude, relieved when one wishes by food, wine, and good company in the bar and dining room four decks below, I am somehow complete. In the sea rhythm and the wind on deck, I fill my lungs with ocean emptiness and the pure wind circling the Earth; in hard weather, driven below, I kneel on the spare bunk and peer out of my window at the waves, awaiting the passage of light-boned ocean birds in their fragility and their taut strength, astonished anew by those ancient adaptations that align them with the elements so that waves, wind, and wings all move as one. And to the degree that I am able to let go of mind and body and escape all boundaries, I soar with them in the unity of being.

LAST EVENING THE TEMPERATURE dropped 3°C as the *K* crossed the Polar Front and forged into the Antarctic's frigid waters. Though making good time across the wind, the ship must tend southeast, off her true course, to evade the heavy icepack that accumulates at the Balleny Islands, named for the British sealer John Balleny, thought to have been first to set foot on terra firma south of the Antarctic Circle; it was Balleny who warned Ross about ice conditions that might impede him in following the 170th meridian toward the south.[23] Seeking the south magnetic pole, Ross followed the 172nd meridian instead, and we shall, too.[24] However, the ship's course must allow for that West Wind Drift, that mighty river, which in each second moves an estimated 130 million cubic meters of frigid water, west to east around the polar continent. This morning, a 35-knot wind drives the icy fog, and whitecaps coalesce in hissing fans and plumes, casting lace blankets down the iron walls that fall away forever into the mists.

Sea ice can spread a thousand miles offshore by the end of the southern winter. Here in the western Pacific quadrant in an average year, the pack extends north to about 62° south latitude: The solid pack at its September-October peak in the austral spring effectively doubles the huge area of the white world. Locking away long stretches of continental coastline all year-round, a million square miles of ice may survive the summer, as is often the case at the Balleny Islands (where the *K* was briefly trapped by ice only last year) and along the coast of Adélie Land in East Antarctica where the French research station named for Dumont d'Urville is located. Perhaps this explains why Wilkes, Bellingshausen, and "DuDu" (as the British nicknamed that distinguished Frenchman who is credited with the discovery of the Venus de Milo) could never approach the mainland close enough to step ashore. Excepting a few gravel points and wind-bared ridges on the northern peninsula and here and there in the Ross and Weddell Seas, there are few locations on the whole circumference of the continent where the stem of a ship's boat may scrape the gravel.

Aware of the tectonic kingdoms far beneath the hull, my mind returns to the great rifting, the vast slow cataclysm, that separated Australasia from Antarctica—the tilt and shudder (as I imagine it), the huge and sluggish bubbles of freed gases, the long ages of rumbling from undersea.

In the early Cretaceous period (144 million to 99 million years ago), as we have seen, an immense range known to geologists as the Antarctandean Mountains was the more or less unbroken spine of a single supercontinent, from the Andes south through the Antarctic Peninsula and west through the 2,000-mile Transantarctic Mountains, all around the southern rim of the Pacific, then north again through the eastern coast range of Australia, which later broke away to form New Zealand.

Unlike Australia, not a thousand miles away, New Zealand had neither marsupials nor monotremes, nor any terrestrial animal of any kind, having split from Australia some 80 million years ago, before that continent was colonized by the Gondwanan mammals. Even bats arrived in New Zealand only recently, in the past few thousand years, though man and his dogs and rodents would soon follow. As the southern point of what anthropologists know as the Polynesian triangle—the other points are Hawaii and Easter Island—New Zealand was the last large land on Earth, north of Antarctica, to be located and settled by mankind.

On the other hand, the first penguinlike birds appeared on Southern Ocean coasts, with their greatest development in the New Zealand region, where the absence of terrestrial predators made this isolated archipelago an ideal place for a flightless life-form to develop. The earliest fossil evidence of extinct penguins—32 species, dating from the late Eocene, 55 million to 34 million years ago—comes from Antarctica, Australia, and New Zealand, and the fossils show that this family has changed little in 45 million years. Even today, New Zealand and its islands claim the highest diversity of penguins, fossil and living.

"Neither fish, flesh, nor fowl is the penguin," Herman Melville wrote. "On land it stumps, afloat it sculls, in the air it flops. Nature keeps this ungainly child hidden away at the end of the Earth." But as George Gaylord Simpson noted in his fine monograph[25] on the family, the penguins are not primitive bird ancestors as was formerly supposed but the reverse, being evolved from flying birds and highly specialized. We now know that these flightless creatures are most closely related to the albatross and other gale birds, which are surely among the most consummate fliers in the bird world; these two families share special glands for salt elimination that permit them to live far at sea far longer than other seabirds. Thus New Zealand and its islands, in addition to their penguins, are the great stronghold of albatrosses, with no fewer than 12 resident breeding species.

Appropriately, the prevalent genus in New Zealand is *Eudyptes*, with three endemic species, the Snares Island, erect-crested, and Fiordland penguins: *Eudyptes* is generally accepted as the penguin genus with closest affinities to the gale birds. A fourth endemic is the yellow-eyed penguin, one of the rarest of its family due to habitat destruction, which has decimated many flightless ground-nesting species; we were to admire this bizarre woodland-nesting bird at Enderby Island in the Aucklands on the return journey.

One may hypothesize, at least, that over time, some early penguins were drawn southward by the swarming krill and fishes of the polar seas, adapting to ever more frigid conditions by exploiting a new ecological niche in the icy water, and that the great emperor at the bottom of the world was originally a population of ancestral king penguins whose adaptations to the cold and darkness came to include its extraordinary nesting cycle. The emperor penguin's greater size seems to illustrate the ecological principle known as Bergmann's Rule, which stipulates that creatures living in cold climates tend to be larger than close relatives of warmer climates, since the smaller form—in this instance, the king—has a smaller heat-producing engine relative to its heat-losing surface area. Perhaps this explains why, to my eye, at least, the king penguins of green Macquarie are slightly smaller than their peers on white South Georgia, which lies on the Antarctic side of the polar front in colder water of differing salinity and prey species.

INTO THE ICE

The first ice encountered on this voyage, seen through my trusty porthole at six o'clock this morning, is a sprinkling of ice fragments like a crystallized, shattered sheet. The first iceberg, ghostly in the mist, is a snow-crested apparition perhaps four miles off the port bow whose visible section is the size of an immense stadium—a stadium that rises ten stories at least above the ocean surface and descends a like distance below.

Shortly after 9 a.m., our southeasterly course is returned due south toward Terra Nova Bay, which is almost four times farther from Tasmania than was the Peninsula from Tierra del Fuego. By late morning, the sea ahead is patterned white, and soon thereafter the *K* enters the ice at a degree of latitude close to our southernmost position on the peninsula a few years ago.

Even here at the ice edges, the pack appears congested. As seawater freezes and the air grows colder, a greasy mush called "brash ice" forms, damping down the wind chop on the ocean surface and permitting the brash to thicken into scalloped disks like lily pads. Where wind permits, these disks merge in fragile floes, which eventually become new ice, up to three feet thick in its first year. Under certain conditions, new ice can grow and spread at the astonishing rate of 23 square miles per minute; once it thickens into floes, this sea ice is called pack ice or "the pack." In this season, this far north, the eroding floes are readily pushed aside, being separated by open leads or channels; farther south, we will have harder going.

As a child, I thought icebreakers were built with sharp prows studded with saw teeth. In fact, these ships have spoon bows and a raked stem so that the ship rides up onto the ice, using the hull's weight to crack it. The broken floe is pushed down and back to the lower prow, which is scalloped aft to throw the chunks out to the side, the better to open an unobstructed channel. This excellent innovation was first put to use on the Norwegian vessel *Fram*

("Forward"), whose revolutionary hull was designed for the pioneer Arctic explorer Fridtjof Nansen. The first man to cross the Greenland Ice Cap in 1888, Nansen almost succeeded in reaching the North Pole in 1893-96 by intentionally trapping his tough *Fram* in the pack, to be carried northward on the currents. Unlike Shackleton's ill-fated *Endurance* 20 years later, the *Fram* had a round hull that would pop her up out of the ice before it could crush her, one of the reasons she was borrowed by Roald Amundsen for his South Pole expedition of 1911.

The *K* is powered by six diesel-electric generators of 24,000 horsepower total, of which three are currently in use, one for each shaft. The big propellers and big rudder, guided by gyrocompass from the bridge, are protected by metal shields installed just forward of the propellers to shunt heavy ice chunks aside. A polymer coating on the hull speeds the ship's passage through the ice; to the same end, "bubbler" devices force layers of bubbles aft along the hull, cutting down friction, much as their odd bubble sheen speeds the swimming penguins. Thus fortified, the *K* may breast large compact floes three to five feet deep.

Inevitably the pack will thicken, since the 25-knot wind out of the north that drives the ship toward the Ross Sea also compresses the drifting ice, slowing her passage. Heavy snow on the pack makes progress still more difficult, and so does a "close pack" with few leads. A surface nine-tenths frozen would forbid entry to most ships, and "compact pack," in which no water is visible, will halt this polar icebreaker: It cannot be broken and pushed aside since, in effect, it has no place to go.

With no loss of speed, the *K* plows straight ahead, parting the floes. The rolling of her superstructure has ended, replaced by the heavy thudding of steel against ice and the rumble of "growler" ice along her hull. Her sudden stability in the pack is a merciful reprieve to the few passengers still feeling seasick, including the young interpreter for the Taiwan group, the delightful Miss Chin Cheng of Tai Chung, who has somehow managed to look pretty and cheerful on those rare occasions when she appears at all.

An elder in the Chinese group is Dr. Wu Li-Te, who scarcely emerges from his cabin in the first fortnight of the voyage. Miss Chin confides that Dr. Wu, a revered healer, will surely be renewed and reinvigorated in the clarity and simplicity of the ice, which will realign the axes of his being and revitalize his *chi*, restoring balance, harmony, and a sense of wholeness. This cure will almost certainly offset the inevitable despair that accompanies the aging and deterioration of mind and body—or so I am assured by young, bright-eyed, and ever so harmonized Miss Chin Cheng of Tai Chung.

Whatever his unbalanced state when he slipped aboard and secluded himself in his cabin, I can testify (now that we have met) that the intense Dr. Wu is balanced, clear-eyed, wiry, and quick here in the austral latitudes. I am, too, although I dissipate my *chi* with polluting alcohols, which he does not. Handling the ship's brawny roll many times each day as I swing up and down the inside stairs and outside ladders of the seven decks between main deck and bridge roof, I feel not only balanced but unusually fit, if I may say so, with the wind-burned cheeks of an old salt into the bargain.

ICE CALMS THE WIND as well as the ocean seas, and the gale birds have vanished. Over still open water between floes, a lone *Pterodroma* is spotted—a mottled petrel, the last pelagic species we shall see until the K emerges from the ice on the way north. But, not a mile south of the ice frontier, its place is taken by the polar petrels—the lovely brown-and-white Antarctic petrel, followed within minutes by southern or silver fulmars, then the exquisite snow petrel, pure white with black eye and black bill. A distillation of Antarctic life very similar in appearance to the unrelated ivory gull of the high Arctic, the snow petrel is an instance of parallel evolution perhaps analagous to the striking similarity between the southern diving-petrels and the small auks of the northern oceans.

At home I have a lovely volume of drawings and paintings of Antarctic birds done by Edward Wilson on Scott's first polar expedition. By the time *Discovery*, bound south from Macquarie, reached the outer ice on January 2, 1902, Dr. Wilson was already well started on his note taking, sketching, collecting, and preparation of bird study skins for the British Museum, and his first polar species were these beautiful petrels of the pack.

Peering downward from the bow, I listen to the ice as the floes crack and split into white-blue chunks the size of automobiles and crash and blunder down along the hull. Those overturned are discolored beneath with a rust-red stain, giving the ice a dirtied look, like winter ice in a polluted harbor—an unpleasant surprise before I learned that this stain is the phytoplankton trapped in the forming ice at the onset of colder weather. These ice diatoms are harvested all winter by adult krill that have not moved north but survive on this red soup in the drift ice. In spring, the microscopic life is freed as the restless ocean, assisted by spring melt and erosion, cracks and fragments the ice edges; the single-celled diatom algae that proliferate on its underside feed the krill larvae and are therefore fundamental to the food chain.[26]

Farther south, the 24-hour light of polar summer is already firing a wildly fecund growth, providing food for the returning krill as well as the birds, seals, and baleen whales that feed on it. Despite recent declines, the krill biomass of the southern oceans, estimated at 1.3 billion tons, is four times the appalling biomass of the world's human beings—somehow a comforting statistic.

AT NOON, THE SHIP'S POSITION is 64° 9 minutes south latitude. The first polar seal observed is a crab-eater of warm wheaten color, sunning its belly on a passing floe. At 12:25, as I turn to quit the bow, my eye is caught by something on the ice off to the west. And there it is! The stately creature upright on its floe is none other than the emperor of penguins.

I yell and wave at Tony Pym and other birders who peer down from the bridge windows seven decks above. Greg Lasley, hearing my cry, rises from his sickbed—he is stricken with flu—and reels to his porthole in time to see it, but his roommate, Victor, on his way up to the bridge, arrives too late to behold his "lifer" penguin as it passes astern. Interestingly, this bird is farther north than our farthest south point off the peninsula three years ago. The sighting may well be premature, since this species is ordinarily restricted to high latitudes south of the Antarctic Circle. In the afternoon, a few Adélies start appearing, but a second emperor will not be seen for two more days, hundreds of miles closer to the Pole.

James Clark Ross and Joseph Hooker had observed the "great penguin" on their first voyage south, but not until the second voyage, perhaps checked by the northward drifting ice, did they stop to make a scientific collection of this bird, which in those days of smaller human beings came up to a man's belly button if not his chest. On January 11, 1842, Ross's journals record:

> ... during the last few days we saw many of the great penguins, and several of them were caught and brought on board alive; indeed it was a very difficult matter to kill them, and a most cruel operation [they finally used "hydrocyanic acid"]. These enormous birds varied in weight from sixty to seventy-five pounds.... They were first discovered during Captain Cook's voyage to these regions, and the beautiful unpublished drawing of Forster the naturalist has supplied the only figures and accounts which have been given to the public, both by British and foreign writers on natural history. Mr. Gray[27] has therefore

named it in the zoology of our voyage *Aptenodytes forsteri*, of which we were fortunate in bringing the first perfect specimens to England. Some of these were preserved entire in casks of strong pickle, that the physiologist and comparative anatomist might have an opportunity of thoroughly examining the structure of this wonderful creature.

It is now assumed that taxonomist G. R. Gray misinterpreted George Forster's sketch and description, which actually portrayed a king penguin. Forster and his father went ashore with Cook on South Georgia on January 18, 1775, and presumably their description of the "new penguin" derives from that occasion, since it certainly describes the king and not the emperor: "We killed several new penguins blueish-black above, below silky white, bill red [*sic*] below, the point of the upper mandible black: behind the Ears, two large ovated Gold-yellow spots ending in a line under the throat running out & causing a yellow Spot, which is brightest under the throat & faints away into the white colour of the belly … etc." If Gray's scientific description is based on this account, then the first true record of the emperor would be that unnamed penguin gutted and presumably devoured by the Bellingshausen expedition off the Antarctic coast 20 years before.

ANTARCTIC CIRCLE

In the afternoon the air turns cold and high winds come from the low-pressure system that the *K* escaped in her early departure from Macquarie. We are fortunate that she has reached the great calm of the ice, since the bridge reports gusts up to 60 mph. The hood feels as if it might be ripped clean off my parka as I fight my way forward to the bow. Almost at once the frigid blast spins me back aft with a new plan to take cover on the bridge, from where I can admire in comfort the two Antarctic petrels and two fulmars that hang almost motionless in that hard wind above the bow.

Tonight the ship will cross the Antarctic Circle at 66° 33 minutes south latitude—in effect, the farthest latitude from the Pole, in which on at least one day of winter the sun never rises (there is an hour of somber twilight around noon) and on one day of summer never sets.

The Antarctic Circle was first crossed more than two centuries ago, on January 17, 1773, when Captain James Cook, on his second voyage, determined to locate the missing continent, penetrated the icepack to 67° 15 minutes south latitude. When he crossed again on December 20 of that same year in what is now the Dumont d'Urville Sea, he was probably no more than a hundred miles from the continental coast. The third time, a month later on January 26, 1774, he was farther west, near the western portal of the Ross Sea. Blocked by ice without ever sighting land, Cook finally concluded that even if land should exist south of the circle, it must be entirely inaccessible, being covered with ice and hopelessly blocked away. ("I, who had ambitions not only to go farther than any one had been before, but as far as it was possible for man to go ... could not proceed one inch further to the South.") The high latitude Cook reached in that third crossing, at 71° 10 minutes south latitude, 106° 54 minutes west longitude,[28] would remain "furthest south" until sealer James Weddell's discovery 50 years later of an open sea that lay south of the summer pack ice. It seems to me that James Cook should be known as Antarctica's true discoverer, since his third crossing took him farther south than later claimants such as Bransfield and Palmer whose sightings in the region of the peninsula were made well north of the Antarctic Circle.

"In the smallest and craziest ships they plunged boldly into stormy ice-strewn seas; again and again, they narrowly missed disaster; their vessels were racked and strained and leaked badly; their crews were worn out with unceasing toil and decimated with scurvy," wrote Robert Falcon Scott, acknowledging the debt owed by polar explorers to pioneer navigators such as Cook and the early sealers. "One cannot read the simple, affecting narratives of these voyages without being assured of their veracity, and without being struck by the wonderful pertinacity and courage which they display."[29] And Roald Amundsen: "These men [who] sailed right into the heart of the pack ... were heros."

ENDLESS DAYS

Long sunshined nights will bathe us in clear light as the *K* grinds southward. As of today, Werner Stambach declares, the *K* is the only ship on Earth under way south of the Circle. At 4 a.m. the view from my porthole is low blazing sun, burnished blue sky, and blinding white, a burning waste of ice and snow to the horizon, broken only by black lightning-bolt fissures where frigid water glitters like black jade in the narrow leads. Why clear blue sea shines black between the floes I do not know.

The hemisphere of blinding light around the ship inspires uneasy talk about the "Ozone Hole."[30] The sparse form of atmospheric oxygen known as ozone shielded the first life on Earth from solar ultraviolet radiation for 600 million years. In October 1985, in the southern spring, a void emptied of ozone was discovered over Antarctica by the British Antarctic Survey: Two years later, NASA scientists established that the agent of this deadly change was man. Furthermore, it was found that the occurrence of so-called skin cancers (squamous cell carcinomas) had risen sharply in recent years and that between 1974 and 1986, the incidence of the deeper, much more dangerous melanoma had increased annually by 3 to 4 percent. Meanwhile, the hole continued growing, and with it a dread, as has been said, that "man—through ignorance or indifference or both—is irreversibly altering the ability of our atmosphere to support life."[31]

During the dark Antarctic winter, man-made halocarbon compounds that escape into the air, especially the chlorofluorocarbons used in aerated sprays, are carried south by stratospheric winds. Exceptionally stable and near indestructible—most of the several billion pounds produced are still present in the upper atmosphere—they are retained in the high overcast of the endless winter night and activated in the coldest months of August and September, when chlorine and bromine gases produce chemical reactions on cloud particles that rapidly destroy the ozone. The hole widens throughout September and early October, when temperatures warm and the ozone starts to recover. By 1998, however, the rent where the universe shone through the atmosphere was larger than all of North America. It was also very deep, penetrating nearly 15 miles into the stratosphere. By September 2000, the area of the hole, which was spreading northward, had grown to 11 million square miles; for the first time, a large human community (at Punta Arenas, Argentina) was threatened by a serious new risk of cancer.

Without ozone protection, naked sentient life exposed to sun will not survive long. With a stratospheric ozone reduction of about 16 percent, for example, North Pacific anchovies, confined to the top few feet of water, will die in about 12 days; ozone reduction here may be reduced 70 percent. The void threatens to decimate marine life in the surface waters, from the diatoms of the phytoplankton consumed by the krill larvae to the whales dependent on the krill itself.

In early November, with warmer weather, the hole gradually contracts. The winds that maintain its shape and dimensions diminish, and fresh ozone flows in from northern latitudes. By early December, the hole has largely vanished. This far south, the risk of damage from direct exposure to unfiltered sun is small; the Antarctic traveler has more to fear from dehydration and severe sunburn caused by this blinding glare off snow and ice.

Unlike global warming, which went unrecognized for many years and since being discovered has been neglected past the point when its first serious consequences became irreversible, the ozone hole, first identified in the mid-seventies, was diagnosed only a few years later. Legislation to allay it came within the decade, culminating in the stipulation in the 1987 Montreal Protocol "eliminating production and use of ozone-depleting substances." The quick response encouraged scientists to anticipate that the hole might gradually contract, and indeed it contracted sooner than expected. In September 2002, the hole over the Southern Hemisphere would split into two parts, which together amounted to the smallest area since 1988. However, the scientists warned that violent stratospheric weather patterns had caused the split, and that unusually warm temperatures had reduced the ozone loss. Also, eventual progress may be slowed by an unanticipated cooling in the upper atmosphere, thought to be caused by the same heat-trapping greenhouse gases that are implicated in global warming. Even were their sources eliminated as of tomorrow, the accumulation of atmospheric pollutants responsible for both phenomena will persist for decades, even centuries; the difference is that ozone depletion was discovered early and acted upon boldly,[32] in good time.

RISING SEAS

In Antarctic seas, as noted earlier, the summer drift ice is retreating southward, especially in the region of the Bellingshausen Sea and the northern peninsula. Meanwhile, worldwide ocean levels are rising. At least some of that rise is brought about by increasing temperatures that cause seas to expand and hasten glacier erosion the world over: The 150 glaciers found in Glacier National Park on the Canadian border have shrunk to 37, and the last of them may be gone before 2050, by which time the snows of Kilimanjaro will have vanished. Almost a third of the ocean rise, however, will derive directly from Antarctic melting.

In the few years since our first voyage to the white continent in 1998, the world's human population has passed the six billion mark, and famine-causing floods and drought, fires and tornadoes, have swept the Earth. Yet a new U.S. administration unabashedly indifferent to the environment, social justice, and the welfare of future generations has been installed in a sadly stained election largely financed by corporate America, in particular the fossil fuel industry, whose investment has been lavishly repaid by environmental deregulation and a cruel gutting of social programs. Many years of hard-won progress by dedicated people for the common good are being sacrificed to pay for grotesque tax cuts for those who need it least, to our nation's very serious future harm.

Earlier this year, to the dismay of other nations, the new President of the United States repudiated the Kyoto Protocol on fossil fuel emissions signed in 1997 by his predecessor after years of international negotiations commenced at the Earth Summit of 1992 in Rio de Janeiro. The President pronounced it not only unsound, but bad for the economy, which in regard to the long-term prosperity of his country is tragically untrue; typically, he had confused the economy with corporate profit. Though the Senate Foreign Relations Committee by a 19-0 vote urged "the Bush team" to reconsider, the young President's mentors, largely inherited from his father's administration, prevailed upon him without difficulty to give this urgent matter no more thought.

Unfortunately, there is "no serious doubt about global warming," as the *Japan Times* would report in December 2001, during our Antarctic journey. "The only questions are how much is human-caused (most, according to a U.N. panel) and how rapidly it will progress in coming decades.... The great weight of scientific opinion says that climate change is a real problem; the other main problem is resistance in the fossil fuel industries to making the costly transition from the outdated fossil-energy era."

In May 2001, the administration instituted an "Energy Initiative" designed to award more than 27 billion dollars in subsidies and massive tax relief to the prospering fossil fuelers while tossing a half-million-dollar scrap—less than one percent of the fossil fuel share—to alternative energy research in wind, solar, and hydrogen power.

At this late date, as the world grows more alarmed by climate change and unstable weather patterns as evidenced in everything from local water shortages to the death of glaciers all around the planet, it seems astonishing that the energy industries, their kept scientists, and their spokesmen in office still pretend that the existence of global warming remains unproved, despite the Earth's thickening shroud of poisonous emissions; their delaying tactics are potentially catastrophic, more so each year. Here are a few facts one should know to better determine whose science to believe:

The 20th century was by far the warmest of the past millennium. The 1990s were the warmest decade in recorded history. World rainfall patterns are in flux, with more frequent and destructive deluges and droughts, more fires, storms, and unnatural catastrophes, together with ruinous erosion and loss of agricultural lands, forests, and wetlands. In tropical seas, coral reefs are disappearing; loss of the Earth's biodiversity accelerates each year; and everywhere, wildlife distribution and migration patterns are disrupted. Carbon dioxide from fuel emissions is by far the largest component of the proliferating greenhouse gases, and concentrations of carbon dioxide in the atmosphere, already 30 percent higher than two centuries ago, are grossly increasing every year with next to nothing being done, a calamity that our inheritors will rightly blame on the greed and lack of vision of the most powerful nation in history.

As one senator[33] has remarked, the U.S. creates over 25 percent of the world's greenhouse gas emissions while contributing 0 percent to solving the problem. Its obsolete oil addiction intensifies the pressures on stressed ecosystems already straining to support the proliferating human populations. More than a hundred responsible governments have now committed to ratifying the Kyoto Climate Change Accord as a small first step, and a growing number of enlightened companies, led by British Petroleum and DuPont, have committed to wind, solar, and hydrogen cell development in the absence of responsible leadership from the government. Exploring the long-term economic and social benefits of alternative energies, these companies have cut their emissions beyond what Kyoto calls for and made substantial savings in the process. (By its own account, DuPont in the past ten years has reduced its greenhouse gas emissions by 65 percent and saved $1.65 billion; BP® now stands for "Beyond Petroleum," according to that company's latest ads.) Meanwhile, nations such as Denmark and Germany are already converting to renewable clean power; when the smog clears, a number of other countries will have earned a huge economic advantage over the oil-steeped U.S.A., which may need many years to overtake them.

It seems unfortunate that an essay on Antarctica and its geologic history, its wildlife, environment, and climate, should have to deal with such seemingly unrelated matters as environmental deregulation and geopolitics, atmospheric pollution, and responsible leadership or its fatal lack. But increasingly on our diminished planet all challenges and problems are interwoven and finally inseparable. One cannot fully resolve one in isolation from the others, and none can be separated any longer from the welfare and future of our fragile habitat. Antarctica's vast ice cap affects all of the Earth's oceans, all climates, and all weather; it can no longer be dealt with as a place apart. After all, its ice is the repository and treasury of 75 percent of the fresh water on our planet in an age when more than a billion people lack safe water to drink, a number increasing every day.

THE PACK

The *K* is currently due east of the Balleny Islands. With the north wind impeding its northward drift, the pack has thickened, dragging so strongly on the hull that her speed is reduced from 15 knots to not quite 5 even before she reaches the Ross Sea.

By 11 a.m., the pack is nearly closed. From the bridge roof, ten decks above the water, there is no sign of an open lead at any distance. The *Khlebnikov*, bucking forward on three engines, is preparing to use the three still in reserve, for she shudders in the heavy thudding and more than once is dragged to a dead halt by ice pressure along her hull. She reverses, jumps forward, reverses, jumps forward until the ice, four feet thick beneath a foot of snow, cracks and gives way beneath her weight.

Modern icebreakers that deal with compact ice use helicopters to scout ahead and assess conditions. Without them, it would make no sense to approach Antarctica so early in the season, when even in latitudes north of the Ross Sea the ocean is still blanketed by winter pack. On this voyage, the aircraft will deliver passengers to emperor penguin colonies on the ice along the coast that otherwise might never be approached or even seen. The red helicopters on the *K* are AS.350 Squirrels, one of them new and the other six years old but recently refitted; each machine carries four passengers and some equipment. In the ship's small auditorium, Frank Ross, the Australian head pilot, assisted by his junior pilot, New Zealander Simon Eder, provides safety instructions about boarding and disembarking, warning his audience to stay near the aircraft in the event of a forced landing. "Don't believe that because you're wearing a red anorak, you're easy to spot—you're not," he said. In Antarctica, with its sudden, sometimes violent shifts in weather, a downed helicopter is a serious emergency.

Young Rob Fletcher, the carrot-topped copter mechanic, gets a wild cheer mixed with nervous laughter when introduced as the man responsible for keeping these things aloft. One day I asked Rob if it would interest him to pilot one of his machines. He shook his head. "My pay is almost as good as theirs," he said, "and anyway, flying a helicopter is too dangerous to be a hobby; you have to keep at it full-time or not at all." Another day, when I mentioned this exchange to Simon, the pilot laughed. "Rob has no taste for flying," he said. "When he flies with me, he hangs on the whole time."

This afternoon, both aircraft are assembled on the copter deck over the stern, then fueled and broken in with a reconnaissance of ice conditions ahead. The returning pilots offer brief excursions to any interested passengers. Having helicoptered over sea ice in far northern Greenland (and very much enjoyed it), I defer the experience today, hoping to catch up on this journal. However, the red machine's quick jump-up off the deck, the ternlike lift away on the blue sky, looks like such fun that I change my mind and take my turn.

Aloft, one is stunned by the sheer immensity of ice; the nearest land is a hundred miles away at Cape Adare. From on high, the view of our doughty mustard icebreaker opening a blue channel in the white as she plows southward is exhilarating. Simon executes some near-stall high turns, lightly dropping and swooping and lifting again like a gull flying upwind along a surf line. Since he appears sane and seems to be enjoying this, I am happy, too.

This evening, although deep into the ice, the *K* is still 150 miles north of the Ross Sea. A wet snowfall, arriving on the wind, leaves the deck slick. Just after six, in a shifting reach of open water, five minke or lesser rorqual whales, which are drawn to ships, surface close to the hull on the port side. Flashing white flanks, they breach the surface, rolling along like enormous dark gray porpoises; they cleave the black water without raising their tail flukes and disappear among the floes.

EARLY THIS MORNING, our ship crossed the 71st parallel at a point 70 to 80 nautical miles due east of Cape Adare. Her position has scarcely been announced when a raucous yell brings breakfasters to the salon windows to view—our second emperor, not far off the starboard bow. As the towering yellow apparition looms over it with a dreadful cracking and ice tumult, the bird comes to stately attention on its turning floe. It seems unlikely that this bird has ever beheld a ship. Yet it does not flee or even flinch as the great din overtakes it, and flops onto its belly again once all the unpleasantness has passed.

Each day the Adélies are more abundant on the floes, waddling and belly flopping, flipper wings widespread, like little children tumbling in the snow. Unlike the staid emperor, they are scattered by the ship, diving headfirst into the crooked lanes of water.

Gradually the ship is turning west toward Victoria Land (formerly South Victoria Land, named for his young queen by Ross, who would chart this west coast from Cape Adare 500 miles south to the huge ice shelf at the southern end of the new sea). Already the coast is dimly visible in high snow mist that shrouds a ghostly apparition of the Transantarctic Mountains. Two thousand miles long, with elevations over 14,000 feet,[34] this range lies all but submerged beneath the ice that climbs to the very peaks. Three miles high, beyond those peaks lies the ice cap of East Antarctica, a white waste so cold that it seems—so far—impervious to global warming. But all that may be seen of its great ice from 50 miles offshore are remote glints between the farthest peaks, like the fingernails of an ice monster climbing the Transantarctic Range from the far side.

Still well offshore, the *K* is parting some light first-year ice with little difficulty. By mid-morning, the Victoria Mountains—the front ramparts of the Transantarctics—are 45 miles away and its many peaks, including conical 12,500-foot Mount Minto,[35] are plainly visible in the crystal air. Glaciers split by the black ridges of Gondwanan rock fall steeply down to their ice foot on the ice shore. In late morning when snow flurries end, a fresh cold sun turns the new snow on the ice to a glare so blinding that even in dark glasses one must turn away.

Only a small fraction of the Antarctic landmass is unglaciated; the submerged continent peeps out here and there as black cliff face or nunatak (an Inuit word also used in the Antarctic for rocks or peaks emerging from the snow), wind-scoured ridge, a few edges of rock coast. In certain years at certain points where the drift ice relents in the late summer, East Antarctica can be approached by ship, but very few ever set foot on it except at polar research stations served by plane.

Ahead, the pack is broken by big chunks and pressure ridges forced upward by conflicting floes. On a disk of new ice banked by ridges, two emperor penguins raise long beaks to cry out to the heavens in the penguin manner, a lament too faint to be heard over the ship's passage through rough ice. Then, abruptly, the hull grinds to a stop, and the sudden stillness troubles the birds more than its noisy progress. One flops forward, sledding on its belly to the other, where it stands up again, reassured by the company. Its companion, more stalwart, remains impassive, light flashing from the golden wash on its ivory breast.

The ship jumps forward, stops, reverses, tries a new tack before she halts entirely, awaiting a helicopter report. According to Rod Ledingham, this pack in places may be ten feet through. Rather than lose a day or two beset by ice, the ship crashes out some turning space, then bashes offshore toward the east to escape the heavier pack along the coast. Slowed further by a strong northerly current, she is using five of her six engines to make headway. Guided by the helicopters, she tacks, zigzags, bulls her way toward any sliver of open water the red scouts can find.

A silent flock of 25 Antarctic petrels, with two snow petrels as outriders, hangs in the cold updraft between bridge and bow. To westward, from an icy peak where the sun's low fireball irradiates the glaciers, comes an astonishing silver light that illuminates the sea ice plain with rainbow crystals. How beautiful and treacherous are turning floes with their fine cracks, and all the more so in this wind, when without warning they may slide apart, revealing the mysterious black water.

A cold vapor, known as frost smoke, over the ice floes is lighter than mist; it is derived from heat released where wind or currents push the floes apart. As the air turns colder and the wind dies, I imagine I can actually perceive the miraculous formation of new ice in the open pools between the floes, a membrane, wrinkled minutely by the wind, that rises and falls, rises and falls, before ever acquiring substance enough to glaze the surface.

The high stern deck aft of my cabin is ideal for observing penguin locomotion under water. Between powder snowbanks at the ice edges, six emperors race through the sea, the pale gold heads parting the surface to snatch cold air before shooting down again; they bank and turn and spurt ahead on short, swift wings, leaving cometlike trails of those queer bubbles that speed their passage through the water. The emperor, which is said to be the fastest of its family, may attain nine miles an hour, about twice as fast as the much smaller Adélie, the only other penguin here in the high latitudes of the Antarctic. The emperors feed mainly on the *Nototheniidae* fishes and some squid; they may also glean krill under the pack ice. With their sibling species, the king penguin, they are their family's deepest divers, descending 800 feet or more, though dives of about 150 feet are far more common.

In a clear near-windless midnight, the white petrels circle turning arabesques of ice under the fire sphere of our Earth's star, which at sunset, at the bottom of its arc, is balanced on the ice peaks in the west. It will rise again before it sinks below the peaks, for the ship has entered a polar realm of 24-hour light.

UNDER MOUNT MELBOURNE

Snow mists and dark shadows shroud the Transantarctic Mountains to the west. At 9 a.m., the *K* is 40 miles north of the great emperor colony under Mount Melbourne, making good speed through new ice toward the open water of the *polynya*[36] at the northern end of Terra Nova Bay. She enters the polynya in early afternoon, under a thickening sky.

Soon the black headland of glacier-capped Cape Washington juts from the mist, and numerous snow petrels circle the ship, distressed by its intrusion. The small white birds touch lightly down and float like bits of ice on the black sea.

Groups of emperor penguins are turning up in the open water, on small floes, and finally in a long black crescent fringing the edge of the fast ice—the heavy older ice that does not drift away on tides and currents, having become fastened or fast to the land, as in "stuck fast." Fast ice on the coast, usually in the shelter of a cliff or headland, and often miles from open water, is the habitat required by the only bird species on earth that never sets foot on land at any point in its life cycle.

Files of birds appear on the snowy ice, coming and going from the rookeries, as an outlying colony takes shape under the headland; a mile inland, a broad area of discoloration under the glacier that overflows the inner cape is the main colony. With a flock estimated at 10,000 pairs, Cape Washington is thought to be the largest of the 42 emperor colonies, most of them small, scattered here and there around the enormous circumference of Antarctica.

FROM THE DEEP WATER off the shelf, the *K* drives herself onto the fast ice with repeated surges. As the edges shatter, her spoon bow gains the older, harder ice, until at last, on the third run, having penetrated almost her entire length, she is grasped by the pressure of the ice and safely "stabled." (Whether this means she has made herself stable—no more rock or roll—or has enstabled herself, as in a horse stall, no one seems to know.) Within minutes, she lowers her gangway to the ice, permitting her passengers to disembark. A safe route over pressure ridges and through knee-deep snow is scouted by the staff, after which the ship's company is free to make the half-mile trek out to the rookeries at any hour of the day or sunshined night.

The larger colony may extend four miles, curving gradually around the half cirque formed by the high ridge behind the cape and the Campbell Glacier, which flows down from Mount Melbourne. The near tip of the flock points at the open water, apparently because the colony is flowing gradually toward the polynya. One loose gang, or "crèche," of chicks, clustered for mutual warmth as well as protection against marauding skuas, is already less than a half mile from the ice edge.

Even our most seasoned birders, astounded by the riotous phenomenon on this dead snowscape, are fairly yipping with excitement. Ready at the rail in snow boots, doubtless emitting a yip or two myself, I am one of the first off the ship, and I head out to the rookery in my own custody, having learned that rare experiences in nature, while great fun to share, can be leached away and finally weakened by loose talk and exclamation.

Everywhere gray woolly young trail restless adults. In neckless penitential plod, eyes cast down in seeming gloom, they seem to dread some future leopard seal or orca. Some are chivvied along well-worn paths leading to and from the water, while others loiter in loose crèches, all perk up at the approach of large, strange upright mammals in red parkas. Though visitors are instructed to keep a discreet distance, the chicks themselves transgress the rule, hurrying forward like windup toys in that stiff penguin toddle, flippers wide as if to welcome a good hug. Some come within 20 feet or so before mystification gets the better of their curiosity; at which point, they inquire about our intentions in a musical three-note chirrup all but identical to the twitter of their brown kingly cousins on Macquarie. (The unearthly wailings of adult kings and emperors are also much alike.) In its seeming innocence and curiosity, in its childlike locomotion on the ice, the gray wool chick, black eyes bright in a snow-white face peeping out from under its black hood, has no peer that comes to mind among even the most winning of young animals.

If 70-pounds adult emperors, as befits their imperial eminence are larger than mere kings, they are also less regally attired, showing a pale yellow-orange in those areas of head and breast where king penguins display a flaming orange gold. The pink feet are huge, with long, sharp claws that provide a purchase to propel them over ice; the three-toed tracks in the soft snow might be tracks of small Gondwanan dinosaurs in ancient muds. As in the Adélies, the flippers used so powerfully under water serve little purpose on the ice except for balance in rough places; the stiff wing tips, touched down light as ski poles, steer the penguin as it coasts along on chest and belly, using kicks of its short jointless legs and formidable feet, set far back on the body. An emperor I see at a distance, moving flippers like forelegs as it crosses the white plain against the mountains, looks like nothing so much as a huge antediluvian tortoise.

Ninety years ago, at the time of the *Worst Journey*, almost nothing was known about *Aptenodytes forsteri*, and relative to more accessible species, not much has been learned since—or rather, not much that is not also true of other penguins. Like all of its tribe, the emperor is hard-eyed, hard-feathered, and hard-boiled, being no less instinct driven and pitiless than any other animal, not excluding such sentimental favorites as lovebirds, pandas, whales, ducklings, and kittens. It is only in its hardihood, its breeding cycle, and domestic accommodations, that *A. forsteri* is aberrant and extraordinary.

Each emporer or penguin is the solitary product of an extended reproductive cycle that begins in the austral autumn (March and April) rather than the spring. These birds start congregating at the colony when all other Antarctic birds, even the "ice-bird" or Adélie, have departed, following the icepack northward toward the open water. According to Kevin Schafer, a writer-photographer aboard ship, who has seen all 17 penguin species and written and illustrated a fine small book called *Penguin Planet,* the huge emperors are delicate and tender in their courtship, with much billing and mutual nibbling of head and neck. In mating, like cranes and other noble birds, they perform deep ritual greeting bows and vocalize in unison—a "fanfare of loud trumpeting calls," as Kevin writes—to strengthen the pair bond, until that dark winter day in May when the female gathers herself to lay her prodigious ivory-colored egg. Presenting it to her partner, she departs forthwith, trekking and tobagganing across the ice toward open water to forage and regain her strength, feeding at sea.

The abandoned male, which has not eaten during the two months of courtship and will fast throughout two more months of incubation, rolls the egg off the ice onto his feet, nestling it against the bare skin of the brood patch on his belly while covering any exposed shell with a special flap of feathered skin. For the next 62 to 66 days, hunched in polar dark and searing cold down to −40°F, he broods his egg. The emperor's plumage is inevitably denser than that of any other bird, and he conserves heat by huddling close to his male brethren, forming an enigmatic mound that will not move more than a hundred yards all winter. Like the Antarctic cushion plant, the mound presents a minimum of surface area to the elements. Even while seeking the leeward side, each male finds himself spun out to windward to the very outside of the ball, all the while keeping his precious egg up off the ice. Since there is no nest, there is no thought of territoriality—indeed, no thought at all unless it might be a dim wondering what all that fool billing and bowing was about that got this bunch into this bad fix in the first place.

Not until late winter in July, abiding by her strict internal clock, does his mate return. To reach the rookery, coming from the sea, she may have ambled, slid, and tottered a hundred miles or more through savage darkness, miraculously arriving just in time to witness the emergence of her near-naked chick. Even so, she is more fit than the male, which, having fasted for four months, has lost a good third of his body weight. Yet it is the male that has offered its first food to the new chick, pumping into its throat a fat and protein secretion saved up for the occasion in his esophagus; this "penguin milk" will last no longer than ten days. In the intensity of his paternal instinct, he may at first be too weak and addled to relinquish his chick to its mother, but shortly his mate straightens him out and sends him off to restore himself at sea.

After the male reappears, the pair takes turns feeding the chick, which will join others in a gang or crèche in about six weeks. For a time, the parents will continue feeding it, but in early autumn, they commence their molt, producing fresh feathers for renewed insulation against cold winter seas. As soon as the molt is completed, they will leave for good, leaving the chick peeping at the ice edge. Even now it appears that a few parents are moving their offspring closer to the water, squawking at them from behind or sliding out in front, as if to encourage the doubtful chick to follow.

Considering the energy required to bring this one chick into being, their abrupt departure might seem strange, but the chick is already too big to be kept fed (or suffer an attack by a skua), and anyway, its instinct will soon impel it to go seek food at sea of its own accord. Some of these five-month chicks are already frequenting ice edges, sections of which, in the next weeks, will break free as floes and carry them away on northward currents to the open sea; they remain on their floes until the gray down is replaced by the dense plumage that permits them to enter the frigid water in pursuit of fish. In the ocean, the young emperors disperse; where they go is little known. Four out of five may perish in their first year (compared with about half of the Adélies), since even those that learn to feed themselves successfully may not escape the leopard seal or orca. In four or five years, the survivors, now new adults, will return to this home rookery under Mount Melbourne. Those that form pairs will produce a single egg every second year of the long breeding cycle required for reproduction in bitter cold, fierce wind, and winter darkness.

THE PHOTOGRAPHERS ESPECIALLY are delighted by the ship's staffers flexibility in permitting us to walk out on the ice at any hour to observe penguins, and Victor is relieved that we are here in time to observe the great colony before it can disperse.[37] In the sunny evening, Greg and I accompany him to the stranded iceberg that hides the smaller rookery under the headland. Along the snow path, we meet numbers of adult emperors, coming and going from the water. The adults have a portly walk, bowing and calling as they go; exhilarated by encounters with other emperors, they may slap flippers and bump chests like football players. The intense cold light that illumines the white wing patches of the circling skuas infuses the penguins' ivory breasts with a silken sheen.

Icebergs that drift against this shelf can be locked in place by sea ice and strong currents, sometimes for years. Near the moat that forms around the base of a trapped berg, three Weddell seals snooze in the snow; each opens a bland eye or nostril as we pass. Like the emperor, the big Weddell makes its home here in the fast ice, sometimes many miles from open water. As the Earth's southernmost mammal, it remains inshore even in winter instead of drifting northward on the pack.

The iceberg moat serves as its passage down into the sea. In the absence of a moat, the seal gnaws out an airhole, whose maintenance inevitably wears down its teeth, shortening its life. Guarding its hole to ensure its claim on each emerging female, it also defends a vertical territory leading down as far as 2,000 feet to its fishing grounds over the bottom. Its largest prey, up to 55 pounds but usually much smaller, is the bullhead or Antarctic cod (Notothenia coriiceps), a yellowish grouperlike species I recall from the Peninsula, where it seemed to be the catch most prized by our Russian crewmen, fishing in the evening. Like most Antarctic genera, Notothenia has survived for millions of years by developing antifreeze glycoproteins in its blood and tissues that keep it from shattering into ice crystals.

Not having to defend a horizontal territory, the bull Weddell is the same size as its females, which is also true of the other polar seals—the rare Ross seal, the leopard, and the crab-eater. (Compare this with the grotesque discrepancies in gender size seen in the elephant and fur seals of the sub-Antarctic islands, which must brawl over limited territories ashore.) Since it rarely leaves the inner ice, the adult Weddell has no natural enemies, not even the orca. These animals have seen no other men this year—we may even be their "lifer" *Homo sapiens*—and yet they appear indifferent to our presence, seeming quite content to doze off in our faces.

A second iceberg stranded near the ice edge ascends to a high arch capped by a snow dome of sun-filled icicles, and beyond the icicles, against a blue sky where blown snow turns to crystals, snow petrels circle. These pure white birds, as has been remarked about wild fishes, are "silent messengers of a planetary depth that makes us cry out, or go on voyages."[38] I long to know what sense impressions pass through their white heads—none, you say? Very few, perhaps? Limited to human consciousness, unable even to interpret our disturbing intuitions, say, about the trapped intelligence in the eyes of our own dogs, how can we fathom the myriad intelligences of other beings?

To penetrate the consciousness of a wild creature would surely illuminate some vital secret of sentient existence, of pure *being*. On the other hand, why seek to know? The need for mystery, someone has said, is greater than the need for any answer. Better, perhaps to be humbly grateful for those last hidden secrets that science has yet to poke into the open.

A BITING WIND out of the south drives floes inshore that pack around our stern. Here a large leopard seal, dark shiny brown and silver, has hauled out only yards away from the port side of the ship, from where it can monitor those emperors that venture to the ice edge on their penguin pathway. The leopard has an elongated mouth, which it can open to 90°, like a snake unhinging its jaws, and indeed there is something serpentine about this animal, with its lumpy head on a distinct neck. Unlike the no-necked Weddell, whose long whiskers extend forward to detect fish motion in the pitch darkness hundreds of feet down, the leopard is a visual hunter with no whiskers on its naked leering face.

A penguin at the water's edge waits apprehensively as another one dives first; a quick brown flash nicks the corner of my eye and I hear a neat splash between the floes. For a moment I thought the leopard had leapt in pursuit of that first penguin, but no, the flash was a second leopard flipping onto the same floe. Reconsidering this move, the newcomer almost instantly whisks off again—or perhaps it saw me, for I am at the stern rail in plain view, not a stone's throw away. Within moments, it shoots back onto the floe, and this time it lingers a bit longer before departing again in a sinuous forward motion that is quite unlike the wriggle of the crab-eater or the stolid forward inching of the Weddell.

At the ice edge, three unwise emperors choose this moment to join the second leopard in the water by plunging abruptly into a narrow lead where a big section of fast ice, cracked yesterday by the ship's hull, has now split free. Bad move, I think, alarmed for the penguins, yet morbidly eager to witness polar life red in tooth and claw. An instant later, the second leopard reappears with no penguin in its jaws; perhaps it is already stuffed with penguins. Still intent on the first leopard, it circles the floe, repeatedly lifting its head high to consider the other animal from different angles. When again it propels itself onto the ice, it leaves more distance, even slithers a bit farther, before rolling languidly onto its back.

It is just now, as if by signal, that a squadron of incoming emperors shoulder the water upward with the pressure of their submarine momentum and part the surface in a sudden burst of spray. In near vertical ascent, arching higher than necessary to clear the four-foot ice face, they tumble the others crowding the edge like so many bowling pins. Springing up in instant clamor, they flap flippers on their breasts in seeming celebration before marching away up the snow slope toward the colony. (Von Bellingshausen, admiring the jump-out maneuver of the penguins, imagined it was done with the help of waves; in fact it is accomplished by sheer velocity under water and the sharp cocking of the tail at a critical instant to achieve a near-perpendicular angle of emergence.)[39]

Park ranger Rex Hendry and volcanist Harry Keyes, New Zealanders on the ship's staff assigned to monitor visitor impact at Cape Washington, report that the main body of the colony has withdrawn about 500 feet since the ship's arrival and the smaller rookery only slightly less, though whether this retreat signifies a negative effect is not yet clear.[40] A study of an Adélie colony at Cape Royds, on Ross Island, showed that penguin numbers diminished after the first human visits but grew back promptly once visits were controlled. On the other hand, a long-monitored emperor colony has declined 50 percent in 50 years, and others have also declined since the 1970s, including the "worst journey" colony at Cape Crozier, which has been disrupted by too much human activity at the nearby stations, including airplane and helicopter flyovers from the U.S. base on McMurdo Sound. However, the most serious long-range threat to Antarctic penguins is the decline of sea ice and plantonic food, apparently ascribable to warming climate.

BY MIDDAY, a strong wind has grown stronger, obscuring the colonies behind clouds of blowing snow and piling up drift ice off our stern. Slowly the *Kapitan Khlebnikov* grinds backward, crashing free. Sailing south along the coast of Terra Nova Bay,[41] she passes Italy's Terra

Nova research station, perched on dark cliffs under the mountains. Up there among the nunataks, windstorms whirl thick snow clouds into the polar blue.

Farther south, the ship draws near an immense extension of the David Glacier known as the Drygalski Ice Tongue, which extends 42 miles from the coastline out to sea.[42] According to the ship's Antarctic hands, these sheer white cliffs look much like the face of the Ross Ice Shelf—the Great Barrier—and both are fed by the seaward creep of glaciers from the polar ice cap; one thinks of the great Ice up there behind the peaks as a white mass frozen in place, but of course it is constantly in motion. Unlike the shelves forming in bays, ice tongues jut like piers into the ocean, but because the upper surfaces of both are flat and approximately level, either may calve large tabular bergs when eroded seaward sections crack away in storm.

Our ship cruises east along white cliffs up to 200 feet high, which extend unbroken as far as mist permits. The wall is composed of visible layers of packed snow from which all air has been pressed out by the weight above. Strangely, no birds are visible along these cliffs, no penguins, petrels, nor even a lone skua, but from the black water under the white wall rises the glisten of a pod of minke, their spume illumined by low sun. Susan Adie says that the small whales, lunging from beneath with long jaws slightly parted, are skimming the silverside minnows that feed on ice edge plankton.

The ship penetrates white walls by way of a fjord that must have deepened over many decades, perhaps centuries; one day the fjord will split the Tongue, cracking off this outer section. (It is also vulnerable to huge icebergs calved from the Ross Ice Shelf that, moving north on their way out of the sea, may barge inshore on the strong currents and nudge the outer Tongue, breaking off pieces.) At the head of a second fjord farther east, the K drives herself onto the ice to pass the long day's night. Her position this evening is 75° 25 minutes south latitude.

Birgit Bateman's birthday is celebrated at supper with champagne brought to Antarctica by her husband; they are joined by Olga and

Werner, Victor, and me. After dinner, I accompany the Batemans on a flight over the Ice Tongue with Frank Ross; we note two Weddell seals with pups on the fast ice of the inner fjord. Climbing the white wall and heading south across the Ice Tongue's ten-mile breadth, the machine soon gains sufficient altitude to view Mount Erebus on Ross Island, the most active of all Antarctic volcanoes and the highest, at over 12,000 feet; Mount Terror is barely visible to the east of it. Ross named the two cones after his ships, which had been named in honor of his dogs.

Beyond Erebus, invisible in sunny mist, lies the Great Barrier, as the all but insurmountable plateau of ice that blocks the south end of the sea was known to the first voyagers:

> [The Barrier] presented an extraordinary appearance, gradually increasing in height as we got nearer to it, and proving at length to be a perpendicular cliff of ice, between one hundred and fifty and two hundred feet above the level of the sea, perfectly flat and level at the top, and without any fissures or promontories on its even seaward face. What was beyond it we could not imagine, for being much higher than our mast-head, we could not see anything except the summit of a lofty range of mountains extending to the southward.... We might with equal chances of success try to sail through the cliffs of Dover, as to penetrate such a mass.
>
> —JAMES CLARK ROSS, JANUARY 28, 1841

Grounded on bedrock here and there, the Ross Ice Shelf is an enormous platform of floating ice enclosed and stabilized in its own bay by mountains on three sides. Though larger than France, it is essentially no more than a low-altitude plateau fed by the huge glaciers that descend from an ice cap larger than Australia. An "immense plain of frosted silver" is what Ross called what could be seen of it, presumably from offshore on the ship's masthead, for he never climbed its formidable wall. Ross coasted the Barrier, traveling some 250 miles east of Cape Crozier.[43] On his return, he witnessed an eruption of Mount Erebus and ventured into a bay or sound that he named for the *Terror*'s 2nd Officer, Mr. McMurdo.

Ross's discovery of the Great Barrier and the huge ice sections cracked away from its seaward face provided the long-sought explanation of those wandering ice mountains near the Antarctic Circle that had so awed the intrepid Captain Cook. Because the Barrier's frosted plain seemed to promise an unobstructed access to the south, possibly all the way to the South Pole, it at once became the most important location on the white continent. Yet back in England in 1843, Ross met a cool reception. The continent had now been sighted at so many points that the existence of a polar land could no longer be questioned, yet doubters—there are always doubters—continued to suggest that the points discovered were not necessarily connected by terra firma.

THE BARRIER EXPLORERS

After James Clark Ross, more than a half century would pass before man would venture this far south again. In 1900, the barrier was scaled for the first time by a party from the *Southern Cross* expedition of 1899-1900 led by the Norwegian Carsten Borchgrevink, which included the Tasmanian physicist Louis Bernacchi. Making a sledge foray across the ice shelf, they arrived on February 17, 1900, at 78° 50 minutes south latitude—scarcely 50 miles closer to the Pole than Ross but technically (and briefly) a new "furthest south."

> Nothing was visible but the great ice-cap stretching
> away for hundreds of miles to the south and west.

Unless one has actually seen it, it is impossible to conceive the stupendous extent of this ice-cap, its consistency, utter bareness, and stillness, which sends an indefinable sense of dread to the heart.

—LOUIS BERNACCHI

Bernacchi refers here to the ice shelf; the ice cap had not yet been reached or even seen. The following year, Bernacchi would join Scott's *Discovery* expedition, which landed first at Cape Adare and arrived in McMurdo Sound in January 1902. After an exploration east along the Barrier to what it named King Edward VII Land after His Britannic Majesty, the expedition established a base camp at Hut Point, on the west end of Ross Island.

Scott's closest associate and confidant was "Uncle Bill" Wilson, who was also close to the young merchant marine officer Ernest Shackleton. According to Scott's diary, the eager Shackleton would accompany Wilson nearly a thousand feet uphill from camp each day to record temperatures. In November 1902, these three would make the first serious attempt to "conquer" the South Pole, man-hauling sledges inland for some 300 miles over the ice shelf (and taking turns each evening reading Darwin aloud in their three-man sleeping bag). The journey proved to be so arduous that Shackleton, ill and near collapse, was not permitted to accompany Scott and Wilson the full distance to the new "furthest south" at 82° 17 minutes south latitude (December 30, 1902); upon their return to Ross Island, Scott ordered that Shackleton be invalided home. Considering the Irishman's uncertain health—he would die at age 47—this may have been a responsible decision, but Shackleton never forgave what he took to be an intentional humiliation by a competitive leader he did not admire and had even dared to rebuke during their journey.

The bitter rivalry between these two would intensify and darken the great drama of Antarctic exploration that took place in the next decade. Scott's "furthest south" was still well short of the formidable glaciers that ascended from barrier shelf to the polar ice cap, and a few years later, in January 1908, Shackleton returned on the ship *Nimrod,* leading his own British Antarctic Expedition. Shackleton would pioneer the 100-mile ascent of the formidable Beardmore Glacier,[44] later recognized as the largest glacier on the planet. On January 9, 1909, he bested Scott's record by more than 300 miles[45] before turning back.

Roald Amundsen, who truly appreciated Shackleton's accomplishment (as well as the sacrifice involved in turning back), sent congratulations to the Royal Geographical Society on "this wonderful achievement ... a victory in Antarctic exploration which can never be surpassed. What Nansen is in the North, Shackleton is in the South." Though knighted for his feat, Sir Ernest was not invited to accompany Commander Scott on his *Terra Nova* expedition of 1911-14.

Neither Scott nor Shackleton had made the most of Fridtjof Nansen's advice to depend on sled dogs for polar travel. Amundsen, in 1911, knew better. Setting off in October 1911, weeks ahead of Scott, from a point on the Barrier 60 miles closer to the Pole than the British base at Ross Island, the Norwegian made a new climb from the ice shelf up the Axel Heiberg Glacier, then launched a swift transit to the Pole, skimming over the ice plateau with light sleds, well-trained dogs, and experienced skiers who made the most of the special tents, cooking utensils, and Inuit seal-fur clothing developed by Nansen.

Amundsen's abounding dogs had astounded a party from the *Terra Nova* expedition, which ran across the *Fram* while exploring a shallow bay in the ice wall not far from the place where Borchgrevink had climbed the Barrier. The *Discovery* expedition in 1902 had called it Balloon Bight, but six years later when *Nimrod* appeared, this section of the ice shelf had calved away, leaving a wide embayment that Shackleton called the "Bay of Whales," it being "a veritable playground of these monsters." This was the place

Amundsen would choose as his base camp for his own expedition to the Pole.

To one degree or another, the British expeditions had put themselves at a fatal disadvantage with their peculiar dependence on man-hauling. Scott in particular seems to have convinced himself that using dog sleds and learning to ski properly were un-British and unfair if not downright unmanly. "In my mind," Scott wrote, "no journey ever made with dogs can approach the height of that fine conception which is realized when a party of men go forth to face hardships, dangers, and difficulties with their own unaided efforts.... Surely in this case the conquest is more nobly and splendidly won."

One small detail might stand for all that was inept in his doomed expedition. On the return trek, though full daylight was inescapable for 24 hours a day, and though Wilson especially was suffering the agonies of snow blindness, the polar party never chose to brave the cold night and travel north with the sun behind them. "Nobly and splendidly" they would perish on the Beardmore Glacier, only 11 geographical miles short of a supply depot and 140 from their Hut Point camp.[46]

In the following spring, a search party spotted a bamboo pole sticking up from the snowdrifted tent containing the frozen bodies of Birdie Bowers, "Bill" Wilson, and Captain Scott, whose arm broke with a loud snap when his body was shifted in order to retrieve the celebrated journal and last letters. "Their skin was yellow and glassy, like old alabaster," wrote Cherry-Garrard, who helped bury the three men in the tent under a snow cairn. (The bodies of Petty Officer Evans and Captain Oates lay somewhere along the drifted track back toward the south.) Even today, hard-frozen in dry snow, Scott's polar party might appear much as it did in the haggard photograph that recorded its arrival at the Pole almost a century ago. Moving infinitesimally with the glacier ice toward the cliff edge, the five entombed men may one day escape the Great Barrier, falling hundreds of feet into the sea in cascades of calving ice and drifting north into the oceans.

Out of sight of our helicopter beyond Ross Island lies an iceberg 185 miles long and 25 wide, largest on record—nearly twice the size of Long Island, New York, where I now live. The cracks that would split it from the ice shelf's seaward wall were monitored by satellite for nine years before March 2000, when it broke off in two sections, carrying away Amundsen's base site and the Bay of Whales and reconfiguring that entire Barrier. The first section, called B-15A, drifted west and north past Ross Island and this Ice Tongue, which it might have shattered with one massive nudge. B-15B, which is far larger, traveled less than 250 miles before going aground on the continental shelf off Cape Crozier, where its high rampart (120 miles long) fills the horizon.[47]

Together with the Ice Tongue, B-15B pens ice into the southwest corner of the Ross Sea and McMurdo Sound, blocking its annual exodus on the strong current of the gyre that carries it north past Cape Adare into the Antarctic Ocean. The ice all but blocks the shipping channel into the all-year National Science Foundation research station at McMurdo, which services the Amundsen-Scott station at the Pole. The immense ice masses also threaten the southernmost of the Earth's penguin colonies, impeding the Adélie migrations to Cape Royds as well as the emperor's travels to and from Cape Crozier. Though the channel is ordinarily navigated by a half dozen supply ships every year, its use is increasingly dependent on huge icebreakers.

Just west of McMurdo Sound lie the Dry Valleys, a desert region from which all but a few small glaciers are cut off by the high peaks of the Transantarctics. In a rocky terrain resembling Mars, no rain or snow has fallen for two million years, and little or nothing degrades in the frozen air. Not counting the mummified remains of errant seals that for reasons unknown even to themselves struggled laboriously inland from the ice and died there in mystifying numbers, the highest creatures on its chain of life are three species of microscopic roundworms that inhabit its few mosses, subsist on bacteria, and resist deep-freezing. Freeze-dried algae in the Dry Valleys may be ten million years old, and a glacier remnant up to eight million years old is thought to hold the oldest ice and water on the planet.

Lost in the mists southeast of the Ice Tongue lies Franklin Island, named by Ross for his friend Captain Sir John Franklin, Governor of Tasmania, and former leader of 1819 and 1825 expeditions to the Canadian Arctic. After Ross's return, the British Admiralty assigned the refitted *Erebus* and *Terror* to Franklin, who with Captain Crozier and 128 officers and men would disappear with both ships on a doomed expedition of 1845 to navigate the length of the Northwest Passage; Ross commanded one of the many ships that searched for survivors in vain. In the course of that search in 1854, Captain Edward Belcher would chart the passage, losing four of his five ships in the process. Not until 1903-1906 would the passage be navigated from end to end by Franklin's lifelong admirer, the relentless young Norwegian Roald Amundsen.

Even from the air, no water is visible in the white plain between the Ice Tongue and Ross Island. The helicopter heads west over the Tongue toward its source in the broad David Glacier, which ascends westward to a towering Transantarctic horizon. There whirling snow obscures blue sky and a sun frozen in place fires the high rim of East Antarctica.[48]

That realm beyond those mountains is the highest and coldest region on the planet as well as the most hostile and remote. It is also the driest, rivaling the Sahara as the Earth's greatest desert—paradoxical indeed when one considers that the East Antarctic ice, up to three miles deep, contains most of the Earth's fresh water. Despite the enormous obstacles to tapping it economically, this resource increases in significance each year that unwise nations fail to reverse the ongoing waste and despoliation of a formerly plentiful supply.

(Western governments, increasingly under corporate control, are currently permitting the "privatization" of this most precious of all elements: What man once took as a common heritage and right, like earth and air, will be reserved for those who can pay the most. This unjust and hateful usurpation, should we permit it, will ravage the world's poor in the growing number of drought-afflicted regions, causing unprecedented panic, anarchy, and human suffering.)

Some years ago, it was proposed by Saudi Arabia that an iceberg might be towed to that desert nation, since a single large berg represents many million tons of water, enough to sustain a fair-size city for several years; B-15A, the 1,900-square-mile block mentioned earlier, might supply the entire U.S. for a half decade. But in the end, these monoliths are no practical solution to impending water shortage, if only because, with nine-tenths of their mass submerged, they would go aground so far offshore as to be inaccessible for efficient pumping.

On the Antarctic Peninsula, the Larsen B and Wilkins Ice Shelves lost nearly 1,100 square miles of area during the year after our 1998 visit, and in late February and early March 2002, two months after our Ross Sea voyage, a Rhode Island–size section of the Larsen Shelf would collapse over a few days' time. Other factors besides global warming may have included the heavy tides and currents beneath the ice and the violent katabatic winds, all exerting tremendous pressure on any rifts or weak spots. Much of the northern peninsula, including part of the Larsen Ice Shelf, lies north of the Antarctic Circle, whereas in East Antarctica, where almost all the ice lies well south of the Circle, even a ten-degree rise would scarcely affect the climate. That ice cap temperatures never rise above –7°F, with an average of –40°F, may help explain why East Antarctica shows no sign of melt in this period of widespread warming. Antarctica as a whole affects all of the world's climate, but East Antarctica is so high, dry, and cold that it creates its own weather. Its ice sheet—more than a tenth of the Earth's land area—reflects so much sunlight that it cools the entire planet. Any significant melting of its ice would precipitate climate change, with a chronic increase of violent weather all around the world.

THE ANNUAL THAW and breakup of the ice packed around Ross Island starts in January; the ice will be thickening again by early April. Last season (January 11, 2001) the *Kapitan Khlebnikov* coasted the barrier at 78° 37 minutes south latitude—the "furthest south" of any ship in history, Werner declares. But today is December 6, more than a month earlier in the season, and in this year of heavy ice, our icebreaker will never reach Ross Island, having voyaged as far as the massed pack will permit.

Before returning toward the north, the *K* attempts to open up a channel into the Italian research station on Terra Nova Bay, which is locked in tight by miles of heavy sea ice: The Italians radio that no ship has reached them in 11 months (although the fast ice, more than four feet thick, will support the occasional airplane that freights mail and supplies here from New Zealand). Back and forth the *K* surges, trying to make a channel. With her electric-powered diesels, she can stop and reverse in seconds—not possible with the headway generated by conventional power. The ice, cracked free, is driven seaward by fierce winds that whirl down off the glaciers and steep mountainsides, obscuring the coast in a dense smoke of swirling snow dust. (Antarctic windstorms can build with scaring speed; katabatic winds can descend from the ice cap to the coast at up to 180 mph, almost double the velocity of a hurricane.)

Captain Viktor decides that too many hours will be lost trying to reach the Italian station, and anyway, the ice and winds forbid a landing. Already the pack accumulating astern is too heavy to break through in reverse, a situation that necessitates the bashing of a "turning circle" before the *K* can escape offshore to the polynya. Shaking with cold out on the afterdeck in my absorption in this operation, I am filled with admiration of our ship's light touch in the application of so much power and the centuries of human ingenuity that lie behind the variety of inventions that make such technology possible.

TO COULMAN ISLAND

The ship heads north across Terra Nova Bay, with the emperor colony at Coulman Island her next destination. A pair of skuas quarters the stiff wind, and snow petrels, dipping like terns, search the hard whitecaps and wind-driven waves that break across the floes. Ross Sea latitudes are too cold and harsh for any breeding birds except snow and Antarctic petrels, the Adélie and emperor, and this south polar skua, all of them breeding species and all semiresident except the skua, which migrates north to pass the winter off North America's summer coasts.

Rising behind the emperor colony and the snow ramparts at Cape Washington is the white cone of Mount Melbourne (8,963 feet).[49] This volcano is occasionally active, and its heat explains the phenomenon at its summit, "a few hundred square meters of steam-warmed, ice-free ground where thin coverings of algae, mosses, and liverworts can grow."[50] I am fascinated that among its plants are a moss (Polytrichium) and a lichen (Cladonia) that I have noticed 9,000 miles away in the high Arctic. Perhaps the explanation lies in soil traces carried on the feet or feathers of a globe-spanning bird such as the arctic tern, which migrates south down the west coast of Africa and continues in small numbers to the Antarctic coast. This southern region of the Ross Sea may be too cold for it, but ancestral terns were surely here during Gondwana's warmer periods. How they carried soil traces from the far north without rinsing them off when diving and dipping along the way is another good question.

At last the K leaves the polynya to reenter the crowding ice. On her port side, vast glaciers overflow the Victoria Mountains, which are shrouded in white mists; rock faces loom and disappear. The Victoria Coast north of the polynya is little known even today, say the Russian officers. Since their chart indicates coastal islands that do not exist, our navigators take pains not to learn the hard way about uncharted ledges that do.

In mid-afternoon, off the steep coast where the Mariner and Borchgrevink Glaciers come together at the sea, we make landfall at Coulman Island, 19 miles long, 8 miles across, 6,560 feet high, all locked in heavy ice. The *K* bangs her way north off its offshore coast, which looms through the mist as a black basalt rampart with orange-brown lava extrusions thrusting upward through the older layers. (The age of the volcanic rock that forms this coast, as volcanist Harry Keyes reminds us, ranges from a few seconds old at live Mount Erebus to 20 million years in more ancient formations.) The cliff face rises several hundred feet before it is subsumed by an ice wall that soars a like distance before vanishing into its clouds. Perhaps it was Coulman's rude and inhospitable appearance that inspired Captain Ross to name this bleak rock after his father-in-law.

Greg Lasley has been down with flu most of the journey, which may account for why he (and Victor) have had their fill of whiteness and brightness and emptiness, too, if these qualities define those days when two to four bird species have been seen—"the fewest ever in one day on any bird trip our company has ever led," marvels Victor, as if he had won by picking "low" in a high-low poker game. Greg corroborates this claim in a voice of mourning. For all the astonishing beauty of the ice, sighs Victor, he will never return to Antarctica by this long sea route. Yet he is indomitably positive in outlook, and will later describe this journey as "one of my ten best ever."

ALL EVENING AND all the sunshined night, the ship thunders through heavy ice wedged hard against Coulman's coast; I descend to Deck 3, below the waterline, to apprehend the force exerted by the fearsome crash of ice against steel plate. By 6 a.m., the *K* has gained scarcely 20 miles. Off the north cape, she works inshore through the shifting leads opened by currents around the point, but soon, unable to go farther, she stables herself in the thick ice that seals the sound between Coulman and the continent. In the rigid pristine air, clear as a lens, the mainland appears to be no more than six miles off, when actually it is 15 miles away.

Unlike the drift ice pressing against it, thrust upward in pressure ridges like diminutive chains of peaks, the fast ice appears flat and hard, and the emperor rookery, hidden behind a headland along Coulman's inner shore, is scarcely three miles from the ship—not an arduous trek for most of our doughty passengers, yet too far for the strict safety precautions of the staff, which rightly insists on keeping people checked and grouped to avoid leaving stragglers behind. The choppers, pilot Simon explains, cannot land safely on the ship's rear deck in winds exceeding 20 mph—much less than the force of the sudden winds that yesterday came howling down from the mountains behind Terra Nova Bay. In case any helicopter groups should be stranded by snowstorm, wind, or fog, a trim red-blue-orange tent complete with water, food, and sleeping bags is lowered by cargo net to the chosen landing place, perhaps a half mile from the penguin colony. In summer sun, whisked over the ice in my comfortable air taxi, I reflect uncomfortably on what those first pilgrims to the emperor endured in their winter visit to Cape Crozier in *The Worst Journey,* although not in the least sorry that I was not there.

Crossing the snow plain below, the emperors come and go in long black files like penitents. The Coulman rookery, as we discover, is more advanced than the much larger one at Cape Washington, and big chicks far outnumber the adults, most of which are off foraging at sea. With no eggs or small chicks to pirate, the skuas are reduced to snatching up remnants of fish gurry and regurgitations left from the feedings, picking tidbits from the penguin droppings, and scavenging the flattened remains of chicks that were starved or trampled.

BORCHGREVINK COAST

A wide lead has opened up astern, persuading Captain Viktor to quit Coulman Island in early afternoon, bound for Cape Hallett and Moubray Bay, some 75 miles farther north. But progress is stifled by the heavy ice, and since he anticipates no headway in the coming hours, he shuts down the engines. The ship will drift north with the ice until tidal currents open up more leads.

With the engines stilled, Victor and I join a few clients in a tour of the work decks and engine room led by Vladimir Golenko, chief electrical engineer, a handsome Russian from Vladivostok, who assures me that life there is *"Terrr-ibul! Im-posss-ibul!* No! Even *vorse"* than it was in the winter of 1996, when I passed a few days in his city in the course of tiger research. Displaying the *K*'s six powerful electro-diesel engines, Vladimir explains that this polar icebreaker, though intended for delta and coast duty, is eminently seaworthy in the open ocean, being a rugged, well-built ship that, theoretically, at least, could survive a roll angle of 85° without swamping; the weight of all this heavy machinery, together with 3,500 tons of fuel and many tons of water ballast, will always right her, he assures us. Her water ballast can be pumped from side to side and also fore and aft—not to stabilize the hull, he says, but to *increase* the roll or pitch to give the hull more leverage in breaking ice. In fact, icebreakers lack the stabilizer fins used by other vessels to reduce open ocean rolling, since any fins would be torn off by heavy ice.

Ordinarily the *K*'s fuel is loaded in Vladivostok between voyages to the Arctic or Antarctic; she burns little in the passage south to Hobart since she uses just one engine at low speed. When carrying passengers, two or three engines are used, occasionally more, with an average fuel consumption of 14 tons a day; at the present rate, she can go four months without refueling. This year the ship did not return to Vladivostok due to the woeful state of Russia's economy; she spent the off-season (February to November) at Port Huon, Tasmania, where the crew applied the mustard paint job that must be startling astonished wildlife up and down this coast.

The original icebreakers, Captain Viktor told us later, were built in Scotland in the 1880s for use around Prince Edward Island in Canada. All modern icebreakers are built in Finland. In World War II, the fleet out of Murmansk in northern Russia opened the Arctic coast for convoys as far east as the Lena River; the Vladivostok icebreakers worked the Okhotsk Sea, Kamchatka, the Bering Sea passage, and the eastern Siberian Arctic. In Russia's present economic state, maintaining Arctic sea-lanes is no longer practical—one reason why these excellent ships are available for expeditions elsewhere in the world.

Icebreakers are designed with a notch in the stern into which the bow of a following ship can be inserted, adding weight and power to ice-breaking pressure. Such help can be crucial in the Arctic, where the sea ice formerly remained all year around. The pack has nowhere to escape in the closed circle of continents that surround the Arctic Ocean, and no circumpolar winds and currents to move it elsewhere even if it did. (As somebody has pointed out, the North Pole lies in a polar sea enclosed by continents, whereas the South Pole lies on a continent enclosed by polar seas.) Thus Arctic ice may thicken for years, becoming much harder and stronger, whereas sea ice here will be mostly gone by the end of summer.

When I asked Captain Viktor if he preferred icebreaker duty to carrying passengers, he cited with pride the challenges of ice-breaking in terms of navigation difficulties in river estuaries and narrow channels, and also the dangerous proximity of other ships; he once shepherded a six-mile convoy through the Arctic ice, which he feels must surely be some sort of record. In passenger work, he sighed rather sadly, all that is required of the captain is to be "an actor."

CAPE HALLETT

Cape Hallett [*sic*] is named for a Mr. Hallet, Ross's purser, possibly to reward his foresight in provisioning the *Erebus* and *Terror* for the voyage south with some feral pigs shot in New Zealand's Auckland Islands, which we shall visit on our return voyage.[51] Notoriously besieged by pack ice spun inshore by mighty currents moving north along this coast, the cape could not be approached until three this morning.

From the ship, an astonishing prospect of the Admiralty Range of the Transantarctics encloses the great cirque of Moubray Bay. The day is windless, shining clear, and the ice tumult is blinding. Shimmering ice fields and snow peaks climb the sky, from the glaciated headland of Cape Hallett halfway round the cirque to Ironside Glacier, straight across the bay. Behind Ironside, the snow cone of Mount Minto rises to 12,500 feet.

The red helicopters racket across miles of ice to the large Adélie rookery under Cape Hallett, which all but covers a wide gravel spit and the foot of the scree slope behind. Unlike the emperors, which require fast ice, the Adélies seek out exposed points and gravel shores, a habitat preference they share with their more northerly brush-tail kin, the chin straps and the gentoos.

As Kevin Schafer points out, the Adélies are as quick and active as the emperors are deliberate and slow. Though these two are the only penguin species that breed south of the Antarctic Circle, the Adélie's breeding cycle is quite different. Adélies spend most of their life on the edges of the pack ice, which in winter is always warmer than the frozen continent. In the first light of spring, when the ice pack far to the north is still unbroken, they may trudge and slide 60 miles or more to reach home rookeries on these rare gravel points and scree slopes that emerge from beneath the mass of the snow and ice.

The Adélies at Cape Hallett (estimates of their numbers seem to average about 100,000 pairs) come ashore to breed every other year.

Commencing in September when these points may be under snow, Adélie courtship and egg laying are as brisk as the bird itself, and the incubation period is less than five weeks, as opposed to eight for the massive emperor. Sturdy nests of like-size pebbles are assembled at a prescribed distance from their crowding neighbors, from whom pebbles are stolen at every opportunity in the ceaseless bustle of the birds through the squalling colony. Though superfluous, the extra pebbles are formally presented to the mate, which works dutifully to find a place for them in the rock circle.

The nests, greenish with a haze of algae, are ringed by white rays of guano squirted outward in star patterns so precise as to suggest a mechanical alignment of the nester, shifting from notch to notch while it turns its eggs. Immature nonbreeding birds build skimpy imitations of these nests nearby and do their best to hatch promising pebbles. Unlike the nestless emperor rookeries on the bare ice, the pebble neighborhoods of the Adélies are decidedly smelly, for all their elegant star-pattern decor.

Every nest contains two eggs, white when fresh-laid. Adélies commonly raise both chicks, which keep both parents plodding back and forth to open water. Of all penguins, this species has the fastest-growing young, since the Antarctic summer is so fleeting, with no time to waste before retreating to the pack ice for the winter. (The huge emperor young cannot be reared nearly so quickly, hence the longer breeding cycle, including the need for winter incubation.) Once their molt is completed in late summer, adult Adélies trudge away toward the sometimes distant sea, leaving the chicks to follow in the early autumn.

Heads of small gray chicks pop out when the parent lifts to decorate its star motif with a nice fresh squirt; one chick emerges far enough to peck regurgitated gurry from its parent's bill. Another has tumbled over the pebble rim, and its struggles propel it across the invisible border between nests. While the parent tries clumsily to rake it back, the blind naked thing is pecked by every indignant neighbor that can reach it. One thirsty bird, repeatedly piercing the chick's skin, seems to sip its body fluid—behavior that calls into question the belief that, although Adélies occasionally destroy a skua nest placed too near their own, they never eat the skua eggs or chicks. Eventually the parent loses interest in the dying scrap, which is fated to be trampled flat should it fail to be picked up first by a stalking skua.

South polar skuas nest here and there along the edges of the colony, as I discover when I am dived on by the adults, having trespassed on their territory before spotting the nest. Hearing shrieks, I turn in time to flare them off, but back come these furies and back again, until finally I locate the nest, well camouflaged among the pebbles, and get the hell away from there with face and scalp intact, though not my dignity.

In the few open places between areas of nests lie hard parched skins of penguins dead the year before or even earlier. Excavations of Adélie colonies have found layer upon layer of these desiccated remains, and certain colonies are truly ancient, as shown by DNA analysis of Adélie bones up to 6,400 years old.[52]

In the International Geophysical Year of 1957-58, when the McMurdo Sound base was established, the U.S. and New Zealand built a research station at Cape Hallett, bulldozing this whole spit flat, nesting hummocks and all. The base was abandoned in 1973, leaving behind the battered shacks and rusting oil drums, litter, and debris that disfigure so many polar stations for the poor reason that burial of man's offal in the rocklike ground seemed "economically unfeasible," especially in a place far from the public view. But pioneer visitors reported the mess, inciting a Greenpeace publicity campaign, and a bulldozer was brought back at great expense to pile the litter for removal and break up the compacted ground. Mounds were pushed up to replace nesting hummocks built up over centuries by the penguins, which, being unsentimental birds, soon returned in numbers. All that remains of man's brief sojourn here are a few boarded huts, a large rust-colored cistern, and a small metal shelter with a round porthole blasted blind by wind-borne bits of rock.

Subsequently, stations all around Antarctica were cleaned up, even the largest at McMurdo, which had been dumping its litter and garbage into McMurdo Sound and had even seen fit to introduce a nuclear reactor. The reactor has since been dismantled, but complete removal of its contamination is one of the many hard environmental problems that our governments seem willing to dump on our inheritors, to be dealt with somehow in the future.

(In the early 1980s, at their Dumont d'Urville station west of Cape Adare, the French government dynamited the Adélie rookeries for the construction of an airstrip despite outraged condemnation by environmentalists and world opinion. In their wearisome need to fly in the face of other nations, the French remained obdurate until January 1984, when a mighty iceberg driven ashore by storm put both runway and hangar out of commission before their own commissioning. Awed by such a monumental warning, the French abandoned the project, and as at Cape Hallett, the Adélies, taking the long view, speedily reoccupied their rightful territory.)

Far out on the bay ice between Hallett and the Ironside Glacier, a stranded berg is rotting. Where water wells at its blue edges a pair of Weddell seals has chewed a passage down into the sea. Beyond stands a second larger berg that pressure has fractured like a sapphire, creating two blue faces, and farther still, huge ice masses are grouped in a kind of amphitheater at the foot of snow ridges and wind-bared black rock and the great glacier. The grandeur of ice mountains at Moubray Bay is the most magnificent I have yet beheld on this astounding coast, in part, I think, because it is so unferocious, so snow-softened and harmonious under the sun, just as our spry Dr. Wu Li-Te must have wished.

Before returning to the ship, Frank Ross circles high over the ice, then heads inland straight at Mount Herschel, over 9,000 feet high. Banking scarily within yards of its white walls, he skids his machine out over the Ironside Glacier, which rises away forever between misting peaks. The aircraft heads north toward the Moubray Glacier before banking away and returning across the ice plain toward the ice-breaker's mustard speck, far away and tiny on the whiteness.

OUR NORTHERLY COURSE LEADS past the small Possession Islands where the gallant Captain Ross, unable to reach the "ice-girt" mainland coast, leaped ashore on the northernmost islet. There he toasted his young queen, christened the coast Victoria Land, and planted the Union Jack, to the uncouth jeering of the local penguins.

"At the foot of the hill a colony of penguins (a new species) had formed a rookery. They were in such countless multitudes, that it was with difficulty we could make our way through them; and their clamor baffled all description."[53] This was not, however, a new species but the bird referred to by Bellingshausen two decades earlier as the little or common penguin, and christened the Adélie by Dumont d'Urville just the year before.

By early evening, our ship has arrived under steep Cape Roget, named for Ross's patron, Peter Mark Roget, secretary of the Royal Geographical Society and lexicographer of the esteemed *Thesaurus of English Words and Phrases*. Here a small emperor colony is hidden on a snow shelf of a grounded iceberg that is blocked off by another. Passing through portals of the white ravine between, the Zodiac eases along the narrow channel, until quite suddenly, rounding an ice corner, we find ourselves not 40 yards from the nearest penguins. Standing calmly on the ice in a transcendent golden glow of endless evening, the modest flock of giant birds stands alert but unfrightened. Some approach the ice edge a few yards from the boat and dive through the mirror of the black lacquer surface, only to pop up again close by.

From old snow near the water's edge, we retrieve a lonesome egg that must have been abandoned many weeks ago. How it survived the skuas is a puzzle: Are emperor eggs too big to seize or gobble, too strong to peck through, too heavy to make off with? Dumont d'Urville (and the men on the "worst journey" to Cape Crozier) also found unbroken eggs—a minor mystery. Nested in snow, the solitary egg, in its smooth oval perfection, is pure enigma.

AT CAPE ADARE

Last night the ship rounded the northwest portal of the Ross Sea at Cape Adare,[54] a black basalt headland and gravel point scoured of snow at the north end of the Transantarctic Mountains. Here the ship rammed herself into the ice off the black gravel bench under the cliff. Estimated by Edward Wilson at 200 acres, this bench is one of the continent's largest ice-free sites, not counting the Dry Valleys.

Trekking ashore, we inspect the oldest building in Antarctica, a sturdy hut, about 20 feet by 20 feet, erected in 1899 by the British *Southern Cross* expedition under the direction of the aforementioned Carsten Borchgrevink, he who first scaled the Great Barrier in 1900. Though manned by Norwegians—Borchgrevink was a boyhood companion of Roald Amundsen in Christiania (now Oslo)—the expedition had won British sponsorship, partly because of the recent Greenland triumphs of Fridtjof Nansen. Since this was to be the first expedition to intentionally overwinter in Antarctica[55] (where almost any accomplishment was still a first), Borchgrevink had brought along a rifle "for protection against big game," not yet aware that the largest terrestrial creature to be encountered on this continent was an invertebrate much less than an inch long.

Over the winter, the expedition lost the zoologist Nikolai Hansen, whose cairn is visible high up the black gravel slope behind the hut. Poor Hansen never witnessed the extraordinary migration of Adélies returning to Adare across the ice, which would surely have been the high point of his journey, since Adare is the largest known Adélie rookery, with an estimated half million pairs; the birds arrived two days after his death.[56]

In January 1895, the controversial Borchgrevink had come ashore here in a longboat off the Norwegian whaler *Antarctic,* the famous ship owned by Svend Foyn, inventor of the exploding harpoon gun, which revolutionized the whaling industry, and Foyn's partner, Carl A. Larsen, captain of the *Antarctic* when she broke up in the ice off the Peninsula a few years later. "I do not know whether it was the desire," declared Borchgrevink, "to be the first man to set foot on this terra incognita, but as soon as the order was given to stop pulling the oars, I jumped over the side of the boat." Alas, our hero's recollection was vigorously refuted by his captain, who had fondly expected that this honor belonged to the ship's master, and not less so because he himself had actually been first: "I was sitting foremost in the boat," Captain Leonard Kristensen recalled, "and jumped ashore as the boat struck, saying 'I have the honor of being the first man who has ever put foot on South Victoria land.'"

Borchgrevink's behavior at Cape Adare was used to excuse a notable lack of recognition from the Royal Geographical Society and the Admiralty, which thought in terms of Cook and Ross and disapproved of non–Royal Navy officers in Antarctica on general principles. (These institutions were already invested in the Royal Navy's Captain Scott as opposed to Irish-born Ernest Shackleton, a Merchant Marine officer obliged to depend on mountainous accomplishment and a knighthood to overcome an entrenched snobbery.) In 1901, Borchgrevink produced a book entitled *First on the Antarctic Continent.* In its innocence of any human trace, the Antarctic continent was the one region on the map where a white man might make such a claim—but unfortunately both claim and book went largely unacknowledged due to Borchgrevink's unwinning quirks of character. A lack of deference toward Fridtjof Nansen was the alleged cause of his dismissal as "a fraud" by Norway's mythic hero; on the other hand, the man who reported Nansen's comment was Robert Falcon Scott, who was already preparing his first expedition under the auspices of the RGS and not necessarily kindly disposed toward his rivals.

In 1899, the *Southern Cross* expedition continued southward, landing on the Possession Islands, Coulman, and Ross Island, where a small party led by Borchgrevink was the first to climb up onto the Great Barrier and travel, if only briefly, on its Ice Shelf. Though he finally received an RGS medal, Borchgrevink passed into obscurity prior to his death in Norway in 1934. Eventually, a glacier south of here was named for him, and also an empty stretch of coast beyond Coulman Island.

ON THIS VOYAGE, as a ranger-conservationist of New Zealand's National Parks, Rex Hendry represents his country's Antarctica Heritage Trust, which has duly entrusted him with a key to the *Southern Cross* hut. Since even the humblest man-made objects left by the polar expeditions on Ross Island have been pilfered by visitors as souvenirs, only two people at a time are permitted into the old hut, where nothing may be touched, far less removed. Even those waiting outside in the hard wind, hunched and huddled in the wind like the silent penguins, are warned not to make off with the smallest bit of bone or eggshell, nor odd pebble.

The century-old hut was sturdily constructed of interlocking boards reinforced by steel rods; as a defense against the winds, its roof was weighed down by rocks and bags of coal. A double floor and a double-glazed window with an exterior shutter, paper-insulated walls, and the animal heat of six large mammals, closely packed, held the cold at bay. The tiered bunks are short and narrow (one cannot help liking Borchgrevink for describing his bunk as "an enclosure which can hold its own with the modern coffin"). Worn remnants of expedition gear, tinned food, and a sparse miscellany, including a romantic rendering of a young woman's profile drawn on the ceiling above an upper bunk—otherwise, little of interest has been left behind in a modest space as snug and spartan as a boat's cabin and very attractive to the hermit in one's nature.

Next door to the hut and its adjacent flat-roofed storehouse is the wind-blasted skeleton of another shed built less well in 1911 by "the Northern party" from Scott's second expedition, which was obliged to overwinter on the coast under Mount Melbourne before making its way south across the Drygalski Ice Tongue. Not far away, the boundaries of a rough soccer pitch are still clearly demarcated by lines of well-rounded black pebbles borrowed from the penguin nest scrapes. The huge colony, which covered the level bench and spread far up the steep slope behind, was pungently described by Dr. Wilson on his visit here in January 1902: "Such a sight! They covered the plain [and] the slopes of Cape Adare above the plain.... The place was the color of anchovy paste from the excreta of the young penguins. It simply stunk like hell, and the noise was deafening."[57]

We are here on December 9, a month earlier than Wilson's visit, too early in the nesting season to be assailed by sound and smell. With the first chicks just emerging from the eggs, there is no great stink and not much noise, only a cold wind off the ice crowding the shore. Even the brooding adults are dead silent. The colony has not quite come to life, yet 20 or more skuas are already in attendance, dipping and fluffing in dank pools above the tide line.

At the ship's stern, Adélies leap in and out of the small channel, shimmering with water crystals that sparkle in the sun in a peculiar green-gold incandescence. A shudder, then a "shouldering" of the still water near the ice edge signals a burst of seven or eight penguins emerging side by side; as Susan observes, the escadrille shoots up onto the ice "just like spat watermelon seeds."

ON THE ICE MOUNTAIN

In a luminescent evening, the wind has died and the clear cold is exhilarating. Withdrawing from dark Cape Adare, the ship is surrounded by a white metropolis of icebergs cracked off the Barrier and drifting north in their immensities toward the open ocean, where the circumpolar current will direct them east around the continent toward the Peninsula, 2,500 miles away. Two of the ice mountains have stranded on an undersea ledge that extends southeastward from the cape, and one of these may be 15 miles in length, says Harry Keyes.

Barred by the ice from proceeding southward to Ross Island, the *Kapitan Khlebnikov* is a day and a half ahead of schedule. Werner Stambach feels this may be just as well, since the ship's radio is warning of stormy ocean weather once the ship leaves the shelter of the ice. In a fine gesture of celebration of our last view of the white continent, he asks the pilots to deposit those who wish it on the high table of the nearest iceberg, where sparkling champagne to toast our journey is prettily served by young women of the staff.[58]

To drink champagne under the midnight sun atop an iceberg 200 feet high and 16 acres in extent is pure astonishment. To the west soar ice peaks of the Transantarctics, broken here and there by black protrusions of Gondwana's ancient rock; beyond Adare, the East Antarctic coastline may be seen where it turns away west toward the Dumont d'Urville station. To the east, the frozen pack extends outward forever; underfoot, snow forms a crystal glaze on this section of the Ice Shelf that descended originally from the Ice Cap of the central continent and cannot be less than 10,000 years old.

Under a transparent sky, the nearer vision of snow peaks etching itself into my brain, I struggle once more to absorb the reality that this range of high mountains is all but ensheathed by the icy waste that climbs toward the gleaming pinnacles. In Wilkes Land, on the far side of the peaks, the ice cap may be 15,670 feet, or three miles deep: Its Gamburtsev Mountains, a range almost 10,000 feet high, are engulfed entirely.

On my belly at its rim, I peer down the blue walls of a crevasse, unable to see bottom. The fresh blues in the ice are infinitely pure even by comparison with blues of sky and sea. One day soon this blue crevasse, 200 feet deep, may split its iceberg, destroying its own existence in one mighty *crack.* That a solid creation as immediate and hard as this crevasse beneath me could vanish in a single instant, like some ice-blue hallucination—wonderful!

Below the ice mesa, a white plain without end stretches away toward the north and east. The mustard superstructure and black hull of our ship is a mere blot on the immaculate white napkin. Snow petrels appear and disappear in the golden haze of a night sun that for an hour and a half, as our star inches to a stop, sits impaled on a black pinnacle to westward. The white petrels draw the light to an exquisite point. On sun-filled wings, like doves of peace, they stir dim feelings that I no longer wish to penetrate, since the emotion that the vision brings is precious in the same degree that it remains unfathomable.

And yet there remains "the longing for the ice, the sadness of departure, as if after all I cannot bear to leave this bleak waste of ice, glaciers, cold, and toil"—that yearning to return into white emptiness and ringing silence, that stillness underneath the wind in all its vast impenetrable immanence. "Every man has his White South"—Shackleton again, referring to man's romantic dream of great adventure but also, perhaps, to that ultimate mysterium where man must confront his dread of death in order to liberate and heal himself of longing.

Fridtjof Nansen evoked the polar Arctic "where it was so high under the heavens [where] the air was clean and life was simple ... back to solitude—silence—greatness." For Nansen, solitude and silence, not the Creator (are they so different?), are the corollaries of a "greatness" he does not recognize as spiritual—or not, at least, in Shackleton's sense of "rendering a text," far less "God in His splendour." Yet even Nansen, who argued that life has no meaning, makes a small bow to transcendental mystery when he suggests that what drove men to polar exploration was "the power of the unknown over the human spirit."[59] Can there be a "power of the unknown" in a universe that has no meaning?

"Back to silence ... solitude ... greatness." These words, if rhetoric may be trusted, seem to draw near to Shackleton's "longing." Implicit in them is simplicity, completion. "The air was clean and life was simple." To see and feel life clearly—in other words, to simplify one's self. In the excruciating purity of Antarctica—in the whisper of mingled joy and loss that arises in the heart with humble acceptance of the unknown and unknowable—one might hope at last to arrive at this rare simplicity.

From my cold lookout on the ice plateau—a huge thing as doomed to dissolution as the fleeting bubbles in my glass and my champagne-spun being—I intuit something powerfully akin to "longing for the ice," knowing I shall never grasp just what is meant, however powerfully I may feel it.

THE SHIP WITHDRAWS with effort from the coast, breaking her slow way offshore across the ice plains in search of open water tending toward the north. Staring back at the white continent, I wonder again at the bitter cold and toil and terror and privation that the earliest explorers had to suffer:

> ... strong gales attended with a thick Fogg, Sleet and Snow, all the Rigging covered with Ice and the air excessive cold, the Crew however stand it tolerable well, each being cloathed with a fearnought jacket, a pair of Trowsers of the same and a large cap made of Canvas and Baize, these together with an additional

glass of Brandy every Morning enables them to bear
the Cold without Flinshing.

—JAMES COOK, JANUARY 4, 1773

On our comfortable icebreaker, uncomfortably well-fed, lulled
and cosseted by our hot showers and helicopter service, and never
out of sight of a skilled crew seeking to ensure our safety by shunt-
ing our padded shapes about like a crèche of bright red penguins,
our Antarctic "adventure" seems more than a bit spurious. Yet I
would not have missed this voyage for the world, nor the helicopters nor the high-tech clothing either, if it comes to that, "wick-
ing away," as Kevin Schafer says, in modern high-tech garb for our
outings on the ice. We, too, bear the cold, though not entirely "without flinshing." Despite fleeting intimations of inconsequence and cul-
tural decadence, of being too late for the great polar quest, I celebrate
the magnificent prospect of the ice and our last sight of the white
wilderness that those men walked.

One commiserates with the dead heroes, too, because the hardship they endured was repaid all too often by politics, pettiness, and
calumny. Ross's great achievements were challenged and undercut by
political enemies.[60] Scott was discovered to be fatally obtuse, Amundsen
a ruthless interloper, Shackleton "unpatriotic" for not having sacrificed his party to win the Pole for Britain rather than let it be captured by some foreigner. But who are the chair-bound to belittle men
of hardihood, however driven, foolish, incompetent, and even without scruple some may be? What is this awful need we have to pull the
brave ones down into the mob by exposing their human frailties and
mistakes? Are we so incapable of peace within ourselves that we find
the eminence of bolder men unbearable?

To bite at the ankles of those who risk, endure, and sometimes die
in quixotic, failed endeavors should draw attention to the biter's posture,
belly to the ground. The doubters were not there and they are damn glad
of it. Any ungenerous judgments one might make, even when not

mean-spirited and envious, can only induce an unwelcome regret of those tentative ways in which most of us choose to live this precious life.

FROM ADARE, THE ICEBREAKER will follow the Ross course in reverse. Having sailed south into the Ross Sea, we shall return north by way of Campbell Island and the Aucklands of New Zealand before heading northwest over the Tasman Sea to Hobart. Though Campbell is due north of Cape Adare, the ship must take a northeast bearing to escape the heavy ice piled closer to the coast. It is scarcely a fortnight since her southward voyage, but already the ice appears more mushy and the pack more open. Clear of the continent, more birds appear, to the great relief of my ornithological associates; the scattered Adélies and snow petrels have been joined by numerous Antarctic petrels and a fulmar.

Toward noon, a lone emperor stands at attention as we pass. An occasional minke whale is sighted, and more seals than on any day in the whole voyage: crab-eaters, a Weddell, a few leopards, and then, quite suddenly, on the pack ice not a stone's skip from the churning hull, a Ross seal. Rod Ledingham, up on the bridge, spots the rare seal at about the same time as Kevin Schafer, who comes racing to the bridge from the Deck 4 below to confirm the sighting. I have the good luck to be out on deck when Victor yells from the bridge doorway; I run to the rail for a fine view of a dark chocolate animal, paler below, with an oddly striped throat and a short distinctive face with upturned nostrils. Though it raises its head, this elusive pinniped of the open pack watches sedately from its rocking floe even as the sky-high ship looms over it and thunders past with a terrible ice crashing. (Excepting the Galápagos, the Antarctic—this is not true of the Arctic—is the only place I know where wild creatures seem so unafraid of man.)

What little is known about the Ross seal besides its discovery by the Ross expedition includes its reputation as one of the deepest divers in its family, but its true distinction lies in its extraordinary voice, which is capable of a variety of sonorous notes and trills, and may carry for miles over the ice and under water. Ledingham, an old Antarctic hand, says it is observed more often in the Indian Ocean quadrant, where he once saw 60 to 80 over a three-day period—a possible clue to their little-known range and distribution of this species. He believes it may turn up more frequently with the advent of these icebreakers, which can enter the pack and are less confined to the usual routes and seasons.

Poor Susan Adie, who has made many voyages into the ice and never seen it, had thought a Ross seal sighting so unlikely that she omitted this species from her natural history slide shows aboard ship, and she had the misfortune of missing it today, as did the Batemans and Greg Lasley. On the other hand, they have seen things we have missed, such as those orca close inshore at Macquarie.

Tomorrow the ship might leave the ice and its protection against pitching and rolling, and so this evening after iced vodka and dinner the colorfully costumed ladies of the Russian staff—the jolly waitresses and cabin attendants—accompanied on his balalaika by Grigori Akulich, chief steward, give a lively concert of Russian folksongs. I was sorry to see they were not joined by my deck attendant, Miss Alla Cheremnykh of Volgograd on the Volga River, who enjoys intoning mournfully, "I yam far-r fram hum." Alla will tell me later that she has no voice. Young Olga from Murmansk also declined to join Larisa and Lena and the other gallant singers of the chorus line, saying that she, too, lacks a voice. Olga compensates for this defect with other attributes designed by human evolution to make strong men weep, and these, too, make a winning contribution to a merry evening.

SCATTERED ADÉLIES and two emperors (the last we shall see), the two ice petrels, then the first pintado of the northward voyage: In my binoculars, I capture three striking petrels—the Antarctic, the snow, and the pintado—in one crystalline image between bridge and bow.

At 9 a.m., nearing the Circle at roughly 67° south latitude, the ocean remains carpeted with crowding floes. It is misty and snowing, with a wind out of the east at 30 to 35 knots per hour, but with this much ice, the waves cannot build enough to roll the ship. However, the barometer has fallen sharply all this morning, and the ship's officers predict rough weather as soon as the *K* clears the ice and ventures out across the Southern Ocean.

With a thousand miles to go to Campbell Island, the ship halts in the shelter of the floes to dismantle and store the helicopters as a precaution. Afterward I dine with the pilots, who are relieved to have their machines safe under cover. They regale me with an episode on another icebreaker when a helicopter broke loose in the storage compartment and destroyed three others, all of them brand new.

At 62° south latitude, the last Adélies and Antarctic and snow petrels have been replaced by six species of Southern Ocean petrels and the light-mantled and black-browed albatross. By evening, the horizon to the north shows the dark band of "watersky," which is light reflected from dark open ocean. ("Ice blink" is light refracted from distant ice, as if the ice were reflected by the clouds; it is most intense where scattered sunlight pierces a high cirruss.) The public rooms and cabins have been battened down, with all loose objects stowed.

After midnight, I awake to a bang and shudder of the hull, the first rough weather. But in fact the ship has only crossed a reach of open water, then returned into the ice, which by early morning stretches away into every distance. The wind is 35 knots, with snow. Then the sun appears, the wind dies to a fresh breeze, and ice persists in the curious form of miniature blue-sculpted icebergs. When the ship breaks clear for good after mid-morning, the ocean is still calm, with a slight swell. Adjusting her heading, she sets a course for the south islands of New Zealand.

Two humpbacks and an unidentified great whale are reported in the distance. Victor spots what we think is a Kerguélen petrel, a bird we first saw three years ago on the voyage from Tierra del Fuego to South Georgia; this species nests on remote islands in the Indian Ocean named for Count Yves-Joseph de Kerguélen-Trémarec, who came across them in 1772. The count promptly proclaimed them the long sought Terra Australis Incognita, an error or fabrication he compounded on his return to France with the giddy assertion that "La France Australe … promises all the crops of the mother country, wood, diamonds and rubies." Understandably enthralled, the French government sent him back with an expedition of three ships and 700 citizens to colonize this paradise, only to find that his South France was nothing more than a mountainous dark bastion of wind, rain, cold, and dreadful climate. Though Kerguélen, disgraced, was court-martialed and imprisoned, his name was commemorated nonetheless by the courtesy of Captain Cook. Arriving there on Christmas Day of 1776, Cook claimed the islands for Great Britain with the ironic notation, "I could have very properly called [it] Desolation Island … but in order not to deprive M. Kerguelen of the glory of having discovered it, I have called it Kerguelen Land."

LATE THIS AFTERNOON, EMERGING in slow motion from long, leaden swells perhaps a quarter mile off the starboard bow, then again abeam, then a third time off the quarter, is the great fin of a huge male "demon dolphin," accompanied by a smaller animal, female or young—the third of the three exciting species (emperor penguin, Ross seal, and orca) that we failed to observe in 1998. The black, hard, solitary monolith, scarcely wavering in its skyward thrust, looks more like a portent than a living fin, drawing to a point the emptiness of ocean in a distillation of all life and death.

I stare and stare. What could have been the evolutionary purpose of such an astounding apparatus, six feet high or better? In nature, there are many examples of cumbersome male appurtenances that appear to have no other purpose than an eye-catching display for susceptible females, but it seems odd that social animals such as *Orcinus orca* have not dispensed with them, considering the demands of prey pursuit and ocean distances and the unrelenting attrition of marine life.

Orca populations are currently divided into three groups—the inshore animals in resident pods that range less than 600 miles and feed mostly on fish; transient coastal groups of greater range that subsist mostly on marine mammals, seals especially; and the open ocean or pelagic orca, whose range and natural history are little known. According to commercial fishermen, who regularly report them, the ocean orca feeds mostly on giant squid, sometimes young whales. The animals seen this afternoon more than 500 miles from the nearest coast are the ocean hunters.

"THE ENCIRCLING OCEAN, the spinning of the globe, the prevailing west wind entirely unimpeded; a series of low pressure systems one after the other, like a series of tops"—this is our incoming weather today, as described in a fine new compendium of Antarctic (and sub-Antarctic) lore with excellent maps and illustrations, shown me this morning by one of its contributors, our lively authority on Antarctic history, Louise Crossley.[61]

Yesterday the combing waves grew rapidly all afternoon, until finally the bridge and decks were closed to passengers. With seas still building by the evening and booming and thudding through the night, the ship's angle frequently exceeded 35°, according to the wall gauge down on Deck 4, where the roll is moderate. Up here on Deck 8, where my cabin is located, it might have exceeded 40°, to judge from the fact that the horizon, not visible in moderate weather to an observer prostrate in the bunk—the porthole sill is two feet higher than eye level—climbed so high with every roll that the top of the large square window was engulfed like an overfilled flagon.

This morning brings no moderation, as gale force winds out of the northwest exceed 40 knots. In this ever turning realm of elements, another storm system is tracking this one, with only a brief high-pressure lull between—too brief to allow diminishment of wave height, which this morning the bridge estimates at 13 to 15 feet. Similar conditions are now predicted throughout the six-day voyage to Campbell Island, and also from Campbell to the Aucklands, and perhaps the crossing of the Tasman Strait as well.

Not everyone is showing up to eat the good food still being served on tablecloths heavily wetted to reduce wild slidings of crockery and glass. Each meal is a marvel of pluck and balance on the part of the cheerful staff, who smile in the teeth of all the catapulted wine and the occasional scary crashes in the galley. After dinner, for want of any better plan, most of us take shelter in our bunks in order to minimize the risk of injury, but sleep is fragmented by the necessity of hanging on, and the nights are long.

By noon the ship is some distance off her course, tacking into the wind at reduced speed to avoid the broadside blows of the growing storm. Her location here in the Furious Fifties is already 4° west of the 170th parallel, the line of her northward course from Cape Adare. By evening she is still farther off course, toiling due west instead of north. The announcement comes that the time gained on the Ross Sea coast will be lost before she reaches Campbell Island.

Inevitably a few passengers, pitched dangerously about the stairs, companionways, and cabins, have been injured, one man seriously enough that the ship's doctor confines him to his bunk for fear that his accident might have undone a previous neck vertebra operation. Mistiming the ship's drastic roll, he was pitched across his cabin to a violent collision with the door. There he was struck a second time by the body of his wife; alarmed by his crash, she had left her bunk and mistimed the next wave in rushing to his aid. Before they could recover, both were catapulted in the opposite direction, traveling the full length of their cabin and colliding against the steel bulkhead under the porthole.

Another victim, also felled by his cabin door, lay unconscious for ten minutes; a young woman was hurled right *through* her door by way of the emergency panel at the bottom, but escaped saucily smiling and unhurt. (Since she was seen to have emerged headfirst, a staff member pasted a notice by the hole that read *Don't feed the animals.*) Others go about bandaged and bruised from a variety of minor injuries, the battle scars of a memorable passage.

Having had a few close calls myself, I perversely enjoy this token hardship, which relieves my discomfort over the soft life we have led by comparison with the pioneers of the Antarctic. In any case, I can scarcely complain, having encountered moderate weather almost throughout three previous crossings of the Southern Ocean.

In mid-afternoon, the gale force winds (9 on the Beaufort scale) increase rapidly to 55 knots, or Beaufort 10. By 5 p.m. it is a whole gale, with winds up to 63 mph, and by 7 p.m., it is a full-fledged storm, up to 80 mph, with hard rain and huge, wind-ripped seas—a chaos of white wind and pewter waves in heavy walls that the bridge estimates at 30 feet. Again and again, the bow burrows deep into the seas that crash over the ship, and drenching the superstructure as high as Deck 4 with their tons of brine.[62] Yet within that hour, as if the ship had strayed into that dread stillness in the eye of a hurricane, the storm shifts, the wind eases, lone birds reappear—where were they hiding? Weak rays of sun draw forth faint blues, infusing life into the sullen seas. By 9 p.m., the sky is clearing, though nobody believes this storm is over.

Next day, I check the storm statistics with Werner, suggesting that the 30-foot seas reported by the bridge might not quite justify the term "hurricane" that he had used in his public-address announcements; on the Beaufort scale, such wave heights are associated with a whole gale. Werner points out that although wave estimates under such conditions were, of course, subjective, heights exceeding 30 feet had been regularly reported. All afternoon, the wind speed had been clocked at 70 to 80 knots, and for one and a half hours in the late afternoon the average figure as recorded by the bridge officers in the ship's log was 80 knots, with gusts of 100 knots or better—in short, hurricane.

Whatever the figures, Captain Viktor declares that the wind velocity on this northward voyage is the highest he has ever experienced in the Antarctic. But he also says that his ship can weather a lot worse than the 35-degree roll attained in recent days: "Like that Russian doll, she is *designed* to roll like hell and still pop up again." As for the roll of 85° projected by his chief electrical engineer—well, yes, that was conceivable, he supposed, but since it would smash everything aboard his ship, he would hate to see it.

OVER THE NIGHT, the wind subsided to a mere 20 knots, freeing the *K* to resume her course toward the NNE; she also resumed moderate speed, which had fallen to three knots during the hours she had ploughed due west, heading up into the storm. However, the high swells persist, and the roll, too. At our staff meeting, Werner warns that the weather forecast is still "awful," and that another low-pressure system out of the northwest will probably overtake the ship before she reaches Campbell Island, which is still 200 nautical miles away. A renewed storm of yesterday's intensity might cost us so much time, he said, that we would have to head straight back from Campbell toward Tasmania, eliminating our last destination at Enderby Island in the Aucklands.[63]

Winds and white seas build again in mid-afternoon. Though the ship is still 115 nautical miles southwest of Campbell Island, she is bashing straight ahead, intent on shelter and a respite from the elements in its deep fjord. After dark—for we are now well clear of Antarctic waters, in temperate latitudes where summer night falls about 10 p.m.—I go out on deck to observe the landfall. The mountainous shadow of steep volcanic Campbell Island at 52° south latitude looms in the wind-churned mist off the port bow, and an hour later, the ship passes between headlands into the shelter of the fjord.

THE END

A FEW THOUGHTS ON THE HEROES, THE CELEBRATED AND THE UNSUNG

BECAUSE THE STORM has limited all activities, I spent some time stretched on my bunk thinking long thoughts. This evening I was thinking about Roald Amundsen, returned north by way of Hobart, who by his own account was "treated like a tramp" due to his rough appearance on his incognito arrival at Hadley's Orient Hotel. Today, of course, Hadley's offers an "Amundsen Suite" to the tourist in quest of vicarious adventure, but the explorer's reception in 1912 was a sign of things to come, for Amundsen received but thin applause for his historic triumph in attaining that invisible point at 90° south latitude where compasses point north in all directions.

After the North Pole's "discovery" by Dr. Frederick Cook, then Robert Peary, Amundsen had concealed his new Antarctic destination from the sponsors of his own Arctic expedition rather than risk losing their support; when news came of the tragic end of the British polar party that discovered his Norwegian flag—his "black pirate flag"—at the South Pole, he was widely considered to have deceived the Englishman as well. That bloody Norwegian with the pinched cold face and raptor's beak, so it was said, was no gallant amateur, no admirable bungler, but a ruthless "professional" who had won by means of a sneak attack, cheating poor, handsome Captain Scott of his great prize. (Would the poorly organized Scott party have perished on its return even if no black flag had been found? Of course. And so would the Shackleton party a few years earlier, had it not turned back within a hundred miles of its destination.) The world reaction to Scott's tragic defeat stained Amundsen's victory even in Norway, where his welcome in his small new bourgeois nation, muted by that shadow of ambiguity, seemed more swayed by England's condemnation than by Norway's glory. There was also his harsh dismissal from his polar team for drunken insubordination of Hjalmar Johansen, a national hero as Nansen's companion in the great Arctic saga of 1895-96. The broken Johansen, an alcoholic, would eventually commit suicide, and this death, like Scott's, would be unfairly attributed to Roald Amundsen.[1]

By a great irony, there was actually no need for Amundsen to change his destination, far less conceal it, since both claims to the North Pole's discovery would turn out to be false—that is, Frederick Cook's was false and Robert Peary's was wishful thinking or mistaken or just plain unfounded or—well, false. Having failed eight times in 23 years (including the try with Cook in 1892), and knowing that the 1909 attempt would be his last, the tired Peary claimed the prize on the basis of times and distances that did not survive inspection. Peary's temptation may be understandable, but acting on it was surely more dishonorable than Amundsen's tactical deception. Had Amundsen known that the North Pole was still available for "discovery," he would have left the South Pole victory to Scott.[2]

The controversial Dr. Cook was already a discredited claimant to the first climb of Mount McKinley in Alaska when, in 1909, he recklessly announced his discovery of the North Pole the year before. ("Finally, under skies of crystal blue, with flaming clouds of glory, we touch the mark!") Four days later, Peary would present himself as the true discoverer, recording in his diary for April 6, 1909, that he had arrived there too exhausted to take the last few steps even with "the Pole actually in sight." Presumably he recovered, and was soon exulting, "The Pole at last!!! The prize of three centuries, my dream and goal for twenty-three years, mine at last."—as if, unlike the Inuit and his black aide, Matthew Henson, standing beside him, he was the legal proprietor of this place, or non-place, rather. Certainly the Inuit had no idea what this mad fellow could see in an unbroken white waste, far less what he might be looking for or why they had slogged so far out here in the first place; and presumably Henson, after long years as a black man in Jim Crow America, knew better than to notify his boss of his great error, if error is what it was. In the end, the celebrated Admiral-to-be could fight off Cook's bald lie but not the truth. The figures in his log did not hold up, and neither, it seems, did the silence of his Inuit companions.

Cook and Peary strike me as fraudulent on the basis of their victory cries alone. "Under flaming clouds of glory, we touch the mark"? Surely the rascally but somehow likeable Dr. Cook is making fun of us. And "actually in sight"? Approaching a purely mathematical location in a vast white emptiness, what did the unlikeable Peary "actually" see? Was it, perhaps, that mysterious "mark" that Cook had touched under those flaming clouds of glory?

I confess cheerfully to prejudice against Peary, based on reasons explained some years ago in an article on Greenland Inuit and kayak whaling.[3] I am also guilty of a prejudice in Cook's favor, which I cannot explain at all, unless it stems from the reasons given for the great esteem in which Amundsen held him after their *Belgica* expedition in 1896, which inspired the famed Norwegian to visit his old shipmate in the hoosegow during Cook's imprisonment for swindling two decades later.

Cook would recall that in Copenhagen in 1910, during a triumphal visit before his polar conquest was disputed, he had persuaded his friend Amundsen that going to the North Pole was no longer worth the effort, and that he'd better try for that other Pole instead. Considering the source, this claim invites suspicion, but Cook's assertion seems bulwarked by the fact that within a day or two of their Copenhagen meeting—they were staying at the same hotel—a letter written by Amundsen on Cook's letterhead in regard to buying sled dogs seems to indicate a recent change of destination.[4]

Amundsen's own journals suggest that he changed plans at once upon hearing the news of the North Pole claims in September 1909. "If I were to maintain my reputation as an explorer, I had to win a sensational victory one way or another. I decided on a coup."[5] He later remarked that he could not understand why anyone would be interested in going where others had gone before. But his choice of terms—"sensational victory" and "coup"—suggests a surprise attack as well as a fierce spirit of competition with his polar rivals.[6]

"Although brave, daring, and self-reliant above most men, [Amundsen] shrank from criticism and withered under any suspicion of ridicule. He was, I think, the most successful and most unhappy of all the Polar explorers whom I have met,"[7] wrote geographer Hugh Robert Mill, citing, for example, the explorer's self-consciousness about wearing glasses.

On December 8, 1911, passing Shackleton's "furthest south" at 88° 23 minutes, Amundsen wrote, "We were farther south than any human being had been. No other moment of the whole trip affected me like this. The tears forced their way to my eyes." As usual, there was praise for Shackleton, who no longer threatened him, but no mention of Scott, his immediate competitor, whom he could not have known had fallen six weeks behind him. Plainly he was far more moved by the new "furthest south"[8] than by the actual "conquest" of the Pole a fortnight later, which elicited no "flaming clouds of glory," far less a "Mine at last!" He simply wrote, "The goal was reached, the journey ended. I cannot say ... that the object of my life was attained ... I have never known any man to be placed in such a diametrically opposite direction to the goal of his desires as I was at that moment. The North Pole had attracted me from childhood, and here I was at the South Pole. Can anything more topsy-turvy be imagined?"

That Amundsen had located the elusive north magnetic pole, that he had been first to navigate the Northwest Passage from end to end, that he was a veteran of Antarctica and an experienced polar traveler several years before Scott and Shackleton's first polar foray—all that was dismissed as further evidence of the unseemly "professionalism" that Scott's snobbish supporters used to discount him. Amundsen was indeed a true professional who would remain true to his hard profession throughout his life. In May 1926, with his South Pole teammate Oscar Wisting and American flier Lincoln Ellsworth, he dropped flags on the North Pole from the dirigible *Norge* on a flight from Svalbard to Alaska. Since both prior conquests had been discredited, this one was actually the first arrival; Amundsen and Wisting were discoverers not of one Pole but of both.[9] Two years later, the *Norge*'s pilot, Umberto Nobile, returning from the Pole in a larger aircraft, crashed with 16 men aboard. On June 18, 1928, Amundsen embarked on an aerial search for the eight survivors, only to vanish in the seas somewhere off Svalbard.

LIKE ROALD AMUNDSEN, Robert Falcon Scott was an ambitious, driven man. Unlike Amundsen, he risked and lost his enterprise through lack of unsparing analysis and preparation as well as inflexibility and faulty judgment.

When I first read Cherry-Garrard's *Worst Journey* in 1965, Scott was still a great national hero to most of his countrymen as the rightful discoverer of the South Pole, despite that author's evident reservations. Unfortunately, one dislikes Scott by the time a more recent biographer gets through with him, however much one may pity Scott for having attracted so relentless a detractor. Roland Huntford, in *The Last Place on Earth*, overlooks nothing that might harm his subject's reputation.[10] Yet his comprehensive, fascinating, and very useful book, which draws on strong supporting evidence, including the letters and journals of Scott's own men, is thorough and entirely damning, exposing Scott as a danger to his men, who in the end had little real affection or respect from those whose lives were in his hands. In a letter to his mother, Lawrence Oates, who perished on the polar journey, wrote: "I dislike Scott intensely," declaring that he would "chuck the whole thing" were it not for his commitment to beating those Norwegians to the Pole.

Asked to write an article about what Captain Scott might still accomplish after news came from Hobart of Amundsen's victory, H. R. Mill responded that there would be no results to write about. "[Scott] kept so close to Shackleton's track [up the Beardmore Glacier] that he could discover nothing.... Even if Scott reaches the Pole he ... can accomplish nothing except to bring his party back alive." And Huntford concludes that "if Scott had got through, second and nowhere, with all the evidence of mismanagement, he would probably have been discredited and died half forgotten."

According to another source:

> Judgment of the British Antarctic explorers of the heroic Age has shifted in prevailing attitudes. Scott was cast as a hero for most of the twentieth century, but recent critics have suggested that his only achievements were to write well and to die well.

Robert Falcon Scott is still honored and commemorated at the Scott Polar Research Institute in Oxford, in St. Paul's Cathedral, and elsewhere, including a blue plaque on the white London house at 56 Oxford Street off the Chelsea Embankment that I noticed by chance on a rainy day last spring (2002). Here Scott and his wife, Kathleen, had their habitation from 1902 to 1908, between his expeditions. The blue plaque with which the city of London identifies notable residences for tourists reads, "Robert Falcon Scott, Antarctic Explorer."

That he was. Whatever his mistakes, Scott was a brave man who mostly controlled the "weakness" and "petulance" noted by Cherry-Garrard, and he could be generous.

Wilson is disappointed at seeing so little of the penguins, [he wrote sympathetically after "the worst journey,"] but to me and to everyone who has remained here, the result of this effort is the appeal it makes to our imagination as one of the most gallant stories in polar history. That men should wander forth in the depths of a polar night to face the most dismal cold and the fiercest gales in darkness is something new; that they should have persisted in this effort in spite of every adversity for five full weeks is heroic.[11]

Scott called the emperor penguin expedition of Wilson, Bowers, and Cherry-Garrard "the hardest that has ever been made," all unaware that he, Wilson, and Bowers would die side by side at the end of an even harder journey a few months later.

Years ago the ornithologist-artist Roger Peterson took me to lunch with Sir Peter Scott, the explorer's only child, who was said to have suffered an inferiority complex from the daunting reputation of the national hero he had never known, though his own considerable gifts as naturalist, bird artist, sailor, champion, and sportsman compare very well with his father's abilities. The late Sir Peter struck me as an excellent warm man, very modest, a bit shy, and I hope he did not live to read the revisionist accounts, or learn what Huntford mentions (and I stoop to repeat), that his ambitious mother had an affair with the sainted Nansen in the very period that her husband was off seeking the Pole. Let it be said that Kathleen Scott abandoned her romance when the news came of Amundsen's triumph, followed by Scott's eloquent last note (the one concluding, "For God's sake look after our people"). In February 1913, as the new Lady Scott, the rather well-looked-after widow accepted Scott's knighthood in a memorial service at St. Paul's Cathedral attended by King George V.

ERNEST SHACKLETON WAS FAR more extroverted than Scott or Amundsen; like Amundsen and unlike Scott, he was mostly revered by his men. Nonetheless, he was a "queer bird, a man of moods," according to his first officer on the *Endurance*, Lionel Greenstreet. "I don't know whether I like him or not." And like Scott, he was prey to the patriotic hubris of the time, to judge from the prospectus for his Imperial Trans-Antarctic Expedition of 1914: "It will be a greater journey than the journey to the Pole and back, and I feel it is up to the British nation to accomplish this, for we have been beaten at the conquest of the North Pole and beaten at the conquest of the South Pole. There now remains the largest and most striking of all journeys—the crossing of the Continent."

The "largest and most striking," perhaps, but the "greater journey"? Significant? Worthwhile? Not from the point of view of science or discovery, and certainly not to be compared to the ordeal that its failure visited on Shackleton and his crew in the great saga in the Weddell Sea and Southern Ocean and among the peaks and glaciers of South Georgia, in which, famously, he never "lost a man." Even had his imperial crossing of the continent succeeded, it was at best an empty foray and at worst a stunt to glorify a man who would confess to his wife that he was probably good for little else.

For all his resourcefulness and courage, Shackleton was essentially an adventurer and accomplished self-promoter, and the legend that "he never lost a man" is simply untrue: The Ross Sea party of his imperial expedition lost two men while laying supply depots across the Ice Shelf to the foot of the Beardmore Glacier for the *Endurance* party from the Weddell Sea that was never to arrive. The survivors of the Ross Sea group, holed up in the Scott hut on Ross Island, would not be rescued until January 1917.

Scott and Shackleton were polar amateurs embarked on grand national outings. Because of dramatic failure in their quests, they became legendary heroes in a way that Amundsen, the authentic explorer, never would.

IN THE END, ONE PREFERS the simple men who do hard jobs quietly without reward to the ambitious heros whose victories were fired by a drive for fame and fortune rather than by real exploration and the pursuit of scientific knowledge. The high-flown ambitions of Amundsen, Scott, and Shackleton (which our foolish hearts—or mine, at least—admire without shame) are not what drove men such as Captain Carl A. Larsen, Edward Wilson, seamen Tom Crean and Frank Wild, and Australian geographer Douglas Mawson, to name but five of the less celebrated explorers whose names recur throughout the Antarctic sagas and whose histories particularly attract me.

Larsen, the founder of Grytviken whaling station and a mighty sealer-whaler as early as the 1890s, became an explorer, it appears, more out of circumstance and curiosity than ambition: he was the discoverer of Oskar II Land on the Weddell Sea as well as the historic fossil trove on Seymour Island, which opened up the Antarctic history of Gondwana. As late as 1923, Captain Larsen was pioneering Ross Sea whaling aboard his factory ship, the *Sir James Clark Ross*, which that year killed a female blue whale 31.4 meters long, the largest animal ever known on Earth; the following year, he died with his boots on in his bunk, aged 61, "stern and frugal to the end. Why if that old fellow ... sees you throwing even half a shovelful of coal into the sea he comes rushing down here like a madman. We want all this coal, he says. Why, he goes around the deck picking up old nails. He knows what it is to have no coal, no food, no nails."[12]

Dr. Edward Adrian Wilson, in the opinion of Scott and their fellow officer, Charles Wright, was "the finest character" they had ever met. Apsley Cherry-Garrard, who quite agreed, attributed Wilson's "lovable" quality to his utter selflessness.[13] Far more than Scott, to whom he remained loyal to the end, "Uncle Bill" Wilson was a true leader in both expeditions. Wilson was a gifted and passionate artist— Scott marveled at his close attention to his notes and sketches even when utterly exhausted—as well as a dedicated scientist in pursuit of knowledge, especially, perhaps, where it concerned *Aptenodytes forsteri*, the emperor penguin.

Against Wilson's advice, Petty Officer Tom Crean was passed over by Scott for the 150-mile last leg of the 1,800-mile journey to the Pole; Scott selected the problematical Taff Evans instead. Sent back in the last return party, Tom Crean wept—not out of envy or ambition, one feels sure, but his sheer energy and love of life. A few years later Ernest Shackleton, who had known Crean from *Discovery* days, was glad to sign him on for the *Endurance*. This man emerges again and again on the polar expeditions as a courageous, imperturbable sailor of unfailing good cheer, dog team leader, member (for a time) of Scott's "polar party," crewman in the lifeboat *James Caird* in the 800-mile journey to South Georgia, and the man chosen to accompany Shackleton and Captain Frank Worsley on the terrifying trek over South Georgia's peaks and glaciers to the Norwegian whaling station at Strömness. A few months later, the rangy black Irishman with the leather-faced broad grin was there beside Shackleton in the longboat that went ashore to retrieve the stranded men from Elephant Island. ("I must say the Boss is a splendid gentleman and I done my duty toward him to the end," Tom Crean wrote in a letter to Cherry-Garrard.[14] Returning to England during World War I, Crean at once enlisted for active duty. Tom Crean was the essential Antarctic hero, going home to Ireland to raise a family and open a fine pub called the South Polar Inn in his home village of Anascaul, on the Dingle Peninsula of Ireland.

Frank Wild, too, was a seaman on the *Discovery* who rose from the ranks through exceptional ability and an instinct for the Ice. A few years later, he signed on the *Nimrod* and accompanied Shackleton to his "Furthest South." His experience and reputation as an old Antarctic hand caused Scott to solicit him for his second expedition, but Wild refused, having already committed to the Australian geologist Douglas Mawson's Australasian Antarctic Expedition of 1912. (Mawson, who made Wild second in command, judged him "an excellent Petty

Officer and in some respects more than that ... he could not be excelled in intrepidity.") In 1914, still devoted to Shackleton, Wild rejoined him on the *Endurance*, together with Mawson's photographer, Frank Hurley. Both of these men were selected by Shackleton for his Trans-Antarctic team, together with Tom Crean and surgeon Alexander Macklin. Shackleton put Wild in charge of the 22 men left behind on Elephant Island, and Wild and Macklin would stand at his graveside on South Georgia a few years later. A dedicated drinker who controlled that habit in the field, "Frankie" Wild would end his days as a failed rancher in South Africa, then a bartender at a mine in Zululand. He died far from England in 1939.[15]

Another impressive figure, too little heralded outside of Australia, is Mawson, who had also turned Scott down for the *Terra Nova* expedition because Scott refused to devote part of its time to mapping the "Australian quadrant" west of Cape Adare, a project undertaken by Mawson a year later. His was no glory-bound quest for an abstract and imprecise location to be labeled "the south pole" but a true geographic exploration into the unknown wilderness of East Antarctica.

On December 14, 1912, the three-man party led by Mawson was turned back after Lt. Belgrave Ninnis, age 23, "so jovial and so real but a few minutes before ... vanished without a sound," having been lost down a crevasse with the best dogs and all their provisions except one week's man-rations. In this desperate situation, as the starving sledge dogs weakened, Mawson and Dr. Xavier Mertz would feed them to the others. Mertz, who was wet and sick—his outer pants and wool helmet had disappeared with Ninnis—would succumb on January 7 to serious frostbite and dysentery and perhaps a toxic dose of vitamin A from the dog livers the three men had been reduced to eating. His wet feet rotting, Mawson staggered on alone, arriving within sight of the base camp just in time to see the relief ship *Aurora* disappearing over the horizon.[16] Mawson survived because six of his crewmen had elected to remain behind and winter over in order to take care of any survivors.

Mawson's Australasian Antarctic Expedition, which mapped 2,000 miles of coast and penetrated 400 miles into the interior of the white continent, was called by geographer H. R. Mill "one of the greatest exploratory expeditions of all time." On June 29, 1914, the day that Archduke Franz Ferdinand was assassinated and World War I began, Douglas Mawson was knighted at St James Palace, London. His bravery did not deter the ever-alert carpers from suggesting that the principled Mawson might have engaged in cannibalism, making a meal of the dead Mertz.

NOTES

PART ONE

[1]An English missionary, Thomas Bridges, who arrived at Ushuaia with his family in 1869, was the first to concern himself about the Yahgan. He discovered that much of what Darwin had reported was mistaken—for example, the termination of decrepit elders was not done with an eye to cannibalism but in simple mercy. About 1907, the Bridges family moved north to Ona Indian country on the coastal plateau at Viamonte. There Thomas's son Lucas was to write *The Uttermost Part of the Earth,* a classic account very respectful of the Ona hunters, a tall, robust people come south from Patagonia. This kind family had welcomed me to Viamonte when I passed through in 1959; since then, the last full-blood Ona have followed the Fuegian aborigines into oblivion.

[2]The Humboldt and Galápagos species, already reduced by oil spills and the impact of commercial fisheries, must now contend with prey

loss caused by warming waters thought to have been caused by El Niño, which may be related to the climate change associated with global warming: The Humboldt and Galápagos probably have less than 10,000 pairs between them, while the jackass of South Africa has been reduced from an estimated 3 million to about 50,000. Despite a serious die-off in recent decades, the Magellanic penguin, with about 2 million pairs, is still abundant in southern South America and the Falklands.

[3] Professor Abraham Ioffe of the Russian Academy of Science.

[4] Marine Expeditions, since defunct, chartered the *Ioffe* for this out-of-the-way voyage to Victor Emanuel Nature Tours (VENT), a wildlife safari company out of Austin, Texas.

[5] The loons and grebes are more distant penguin relatives, and more distant still are the supremely aerial frigate birds of the subtropics. Although no fossils have been found that demonstrate such an unlikely link, a common origin of frigate birds and penguins has been established by their DNA.

[6] "Jizz"–(from "giss") a World War II fighter pilots' term for the general impression, size, shape, and "feel" of the flight characteristics that distinguished enemy aircraft. Jizz has been borrowed by field ornithologists for use with birds.

[7] The group includes my old friends Rose Styron, Sarah Plimpton, and Bob Paxton, and also some very competent field birders, including the Paxtons, Andrew Farnsworth, Larry Balch, Jerry Maisel, Donald Dann, and doubtless a few others.

[8] A nautical mile = 1.15 statute miles = 1.85 km = 6,076 feet ; it is also one-sixtieth degree or one minute of latitude.

[9] *Oceanic Birds of South America*, p. 70.

[10] North of the Convergence, *E. superba* is replaced by two sibling species that are far less abundant than *superba*, and other crustaceans take their place as the main whale food, notably *Munida gregaria*, whose enormous shoals may color the ocean red.

[11] *Oceanic Birds of South America*, p. 71.

[12] The same claim would be made for a Ross Sea blue whale captured by Larsen's factory ship in 1923; that female whale was measured at 31.4 meters.

[13] Quoted in *Antarctica*, 2001, p. 150.

[14] *Blue Meridian* (1969), Peter Matthiessen; also quoted in Roger Payne's *Among Whales* and in other whale texts without attribution.

[15] The troops would leave in early 2001, but a few scientists have been coming to South Georgia. Today a harbormaster-postmaster also serves as customs and immigration officer and fisheries liaison officer, and the island's semipermanent population has grown to four.

[16] This is the small South Georgian race of the yellow-billed pintail of South America; another race is endemic in the Falklands. South America's speckled teal is also on South Georgia, having wandered here at some time in the sixties. Like other duck species in marginal habitats, this pintail is omnivorous, dabbling on seal carcasses when other food is scarce.

[17] Alexander Macklin, Scots surgeon on the *Endurance* expedition, who was with Shackleton at his death at Grytviken. Antarctic explorer Erich von Drygalski, a professor of geography at the University of Berlin.

[18] "Gondwana" originally referred to the wild forest territories of the Gonds, a traditional people in central India's remote hill country; one may suppose that this obscure name was given when the primordial supercontinent, still hypothetical, was still a far-off region of the imagination.

[19] The Earl of Sandwich, First Lord of the Admiralty.

[20] According to the *Antarctic Pilot,* the publication of British hydrographers (73 vols.): "The name Southern Ocean has been adopted for all the portion of the globe bounded northward by a line joining the southern parts of South America, Africa, Australia, and New Zealand and southward by the coast of Antarctica." This line is approximately 40° south latitude. However, the 1974 edition limits the Southern Ocean to a circumpolar body of water between the Antarctic continent and approximately latitude 55° south—roughly, the line of the Convergence or Polar Front. By whichever definition, the Southern Ocean encompasses the so-called Antarctic Ocean. For legal purposes, as codified in the Antarctic Treaty of 1959, "the Antarctic" is considered that area of the Southern Ocean and the continent within it that lies south of 60° south latitude—effectively, the frigid realm south of the Polar Front.

[21] *Narrative of the U.S. Exploring Expedition,* 5 vols., Vol. II, quoted in Neider, p. 153.

[22] See "Penguins in Trouble Worldwide," *New York Times* June 26, 2001.

[23] More important, perhaps, is the impact on krill larvae of solar radiation through the ozone hole.

[24] Jurisdiction in the South Orkneys as in the Falklands/Malvinas is

officially disputed by Britain and Argentina, although all such disputes have been rendered moot by the first objective of the Antarctic Treaty: "To ensure that Antarctica is used for peaceful purposes, for international cooperation in scientific research, and does not become the scene or object of international discord."

[25] See *The Crystal Desert,* David G. Campbell, pp. 162-67.

[26] That this species nests on rock islets off the continental coasts was not determined until 1912, by Australian explorer Douglas Mawson.

[27] Quoted in Neider, *Antarctica,* pp. 70-71.

[28] Henryk Arctowski, Polish geologist on the *Belgica* expedition of 1895-96, was the first to propose that the peninsula was an extension of the Andes by way of the long curve of the Scotia Arc.

[29] See *The Crystal Desert,* p. 173.

[30] See *The Crystal Desert,* pp. 50-51.

[31] One clue was the prevalence in all these regions of *Glossopteris,* a late Paleozoic deciduous tree that was dominant on Earth 248 million to 290 million years ago. Besides *Glossopteris,* Antarctic Godwana had small conifers and an early seed-bearing tree related to *Ginkgo biloba,* which now grows naturally only in China. Some of its smaller fossil plants and insects still survive in South America and New Zealand.

[32] In his introduction to *The Voyage of Captain Bellingshausen to the Antarctic Seas, 1819-1821,* Frank Debenham of Scott's 1911 expedition, who served as editor of the English translation, quotes "the highest authority on the history of Antarctic exploration, Dr.

Hugh Robert Mill, who says in his *Siege of the South Pole* that Bellingshausen's voyage was 'one of the greatest Antarctic expeditions on record, well worthy of being placed beside that of Cook.'" This would surely have pleased Bellingshausen, since Captain Cook was his great hero, referred to throughout his journals.

[33] What Bellingshausen called "Alexander Land," a large landmass just west of the southern peninsula, would turn out to be an enormous island connected by ice to the mainland. This stretch of coast, now Princess Martha Land, would remain unvisited for another century; it was given its name by the *Norwegia* expedition of 1929-30.

[34] The *Vostok*, or "East," (as in Russia's easternmost city, Vladivostok) commemorated today in the name of Russia's polar station on the ice cap.

[35] James Wright, *The Jewel.*

[36] On a Caribbean birding voyage two years later, recognizing the same sunset conditions—cloudless weather and a clear horizon—I rudely interrupted Victor's outdoor lecture on the afterdeck, shouting at his audience to grab binoculars and focus on the sun. "Just *look!*" I yelled. Those who dared look saw the green flash—a more diffuse flash, to be sure, since in the Caribbean, even a clear sunset is shrouded by the smog of fossil fuels and can never be as diamond clear as a sunset at the bottom of the world. Even so, I was delighted to see it, if only as an affirmation of that first experience south of Deception Island.

[37] See *Seasons of Life and Land*, by S. Banerjee, P. Matthiessen, G. B. Schaller, et al., Mountaineers Press, Seattle, 2003.

[38] Some scientists say that the seeming disintegration of West Antarctica's ice sheet may be less attributable to global warming than to the "grounding line," the boundary where floating ice is deep enough to touch the bottom—of the early Holocene, circa 10,000 years ago; this line has retreated about 800 miles (at an average 400 feet per year) over the last 7,600 years and has not accelerated in recent decades as has the rate of warming. Others have questioned whether rising world temperatures in recent decades can alone be responsible for the melting of the West Antarctic Ice Sheet, since the rise has been insignificant south of the peninsula. No one questions, however, that the thawing of Antarctica could only be speeded by future warming. (See *Science*, October 8, 1999.)

[39] See *New York Times*, December 11, 2001.

[40] See *Harper's*, August 2001; the article by British Antarctic Survey scientists in *Science*, September 7, 2001; *New York Times* Science section, April 2, 2002.

[41] Edouard Lockroy of the French Chamber of Deputies helped explorer Jean-Baptiste Charcot with government funding for the French Antarctic Expedition to this region of 1903-05; Port Lockroy is now a British station.

[42] Named for August Petermann, a German geographer of the 19th century.

[43] Named for Titian Peale of the great Philadelphia clan of painters, who accompanied the U.S. Exploring Expedition under Charles Wilkes on its four-year journey to Antarctica and the Pacific, 1838-42.

Part Two

1. Sara Wheeler. *Cherry,* Random House, New York, 2002, pp. 107-108.

2. Though Wilson, in 1911, was probably unaware of it, Haeckel's theory was already being challenged; it is now discarded.

3. *Cherry,* p. 117.

4. *Cherry,* p. 294.

5. *Cherry,* p. 114.

6. *Cherry,* p. 119.

7. See also Wilson's laconic account of The Worst Journey, in *Birds,* pp. 159-77.

8. The book would be celebrated by such literary eminences as H. M. Tomlinson, John Galsworthy, H. G. Wells, A. A. Milne, and J. M. Barrie.

9. *Birds,* p. 29.

10. *Birds,* p. 29.

11. *Cherry,* p. 215.

12. *Cherry,* p. 87.

13. In the subtropical ages of the early Cretaceous, small dinosaurs still inhabited Gondwana. *Leaellynasaura,* perhaps warm-blooded and feathered, with large eyes adapted to activity in the long darkness

of southern winter, are also found among the fossils on Australia's southern coast, in the region formerly contiguous with Antarctica.

[14] The marsupial opossum migrated north into North America. See introduction to *A Photographic Guide to Mammals of Australia*, R. Strahan, The Australian Museum,1995.

PART THREE

[1] Besides the field leaders—Victor Emanuel and Greg Lasley, Robert Bateman and I—veterans of the 1998 trip include Birgit Bateman, Russell and Huong Payson (Huong is a lively and energetic conservationist involved in saving the last eastern sarus cranes in Vietnam), and Mandy and Joe McGehee. Also with us is Carol Walton, the widow of our late friend and colleague, the legendary field ornithologist Ted Parker, who died in a plane crash in the Andes.

[2] For information on her Moonbird People, I am grateful to Darlene Mansell at Mole Creek, east of Crater Mountain, Tasmania.

[3] In 1840, "DuDu," as the British dubbed him, returned to La Belle France and was promoted to vice admiral; he died in a train wreck with Adélie and their son just two years later. In 1820, Dumont d'Urville had been the discoverer of the Venus de Milo at Melos, Greece.

[4] Wilkes's elegant remarks on icebergs have been quoted earlier.

[5] See *Worst Journey in the World*, p. xxi.

[6] Pintado, white-chinned, white-headed, great-winged, Gould's, soft-plumaged, and the fairy prion.

[7] Notably Louise Crossley (Antarctic history), Harry Keyes (geology), Susan Adie (natural history), Rod Ledingham (general lore).

[8] The island's foundation is the Macquarie Ridge, on an abyssal plain that extends all the way to New Zealand, 700 miles to the northeast.

[9] See Neider, p. 144.

[10] Other sub-Antarctic islands are the Kerguélens, Crozet, Marion, Prince Edward, Heard Island and MacDonald Islands, Iles Bouvet or Bouvetoya, and South Georgia. The latter three, being south of the Polar Front, are glaciated, and might even be considered as outlying Antarctic islands.

[11] Hasselborough, on the *Perseverance* out of Sydney, named the island for Gov. Lachlan Macquarie of New South Wales.

[12] The fur seals of the Southern Ocean have been "split" or divided by taxonomists into the Antarctic, sub-Antarctic, and New Zealand races. Macquarie is the one place on Earth inhabited by all three races, and the precise identity of its historic "upland seals" cannot be known, since the modern animals live indiscriminately in mixed colonies and 70 percent of them are hybrids. For a time, the Antarctic race was thought to be extinct, and the sub-Antarctic endangered, but in recent times, the former was rediscovered at South Georgia, where it thrives today.

[13] Joseph R. Burton, quoted in *Antarctica: A Guide to the Wildlife* by T. Soper, p. 18.

[14] E. A. Wilson, *Birds*, p. 21.
[15] See *Blue Meridian*, Peter Matthiessen.

[16] The expedition was led here in 1911 by Australian geologist-explorer

Douglas Mawson, who set up a radio station under the North Head, known as Wireless Hill, to maintain contact with his 1912 expedition to map the Antarctic coastal region west of the Ross Sea.

[17] Charles Wilkes's vivid description of an orca attacking the tongue of a great whale. Or R. F. Scott's breathless account of an orca pod bursting the ice in earnest pursuit of the photographer Herbert Ponting, quoted in Neider, *Antarctica,* p. 300.

[18] *Antarctica,* 2001, p. 352.

[19] See excellent description of royal penguins at Macquarie by Mr. Eld, Charles Wilkes's naturalist, quoted in *Antarctica: Firsthand Accounts of Exploration and Endurance,* ed. by Charles Neider, pp. 141-43.

[20] See *The Birds of Heaven,* Peter Matthiessen, 2001.

[21] Although conspecific with those we saw in Tierra del Fuego, South Georgia, and the Antarctic Peninsula, these cormorants differ sufficiently from region to region to be classified as distinct geographic races.

[22] Apsley Cherry-Garrard.

[23] Seal Captain John Balleny.

[24] This course is still well west of what is now known as the Ross Sea corridor, which traces the 180th meridian and has generally permitted limited shipping access in the summer to the research base at McMurdo Sound in the southernmost Ross Sea.

[25] *Penguins: Past and Present, Here and There.* George Gaylord Simpson. Yale University Press, New Haven, CT, 1976.

[26] Besides diatoms, the ice community includes bacteria, fungi, and single-celled protozoans, which feed on the phytoplankton and bacteria and become food for larger invertebrates such as roundworms or nematodes, turbellarians, formanifera, copepods, amphipods, and the shrimp-like krill.

[27] Taxonomist G. R. Gray, who prepared the first scientific description for *Annual Magazine of Nature History,* 1844.

[28] First postulated in 1884, the prime meridian of longitude at 0° ran through Greenwich, in England, north through the North Pole and south again through the Bering Sea as the International Date Line. Crossing the emptiest wastes of the Pacific, the line makes a small eastward jog to minimize time zone inconvenience by passing just east of New Zealand, continuing south to the Ross Sea and the South Pole.

[29] Scott, *Voyage of the Discovery,* vol. I, p. 9, quoted in *Worst Journey in the World,* p. xxi.

[30] See *Antarctica,* 2001, pp. 78-81.

[31] Senator John Chafee (R-Rhode Island), chairman of the Environmental Pollution Subcommittee, quoted in *The Earth Remains Forever: Generations at a Crossroads* by biologist Rob Jackson, University of Texas Press, 2002.

[32] NASA/NOAA press release, September 30, 2002; also *Science Times,* Tuesday, October 8, 2002.

[33] Senator Ron Dryden (D-Oregon).

[34] At the Vinson Massif, south of the Weddell Sea, the highest point on the continent rises to 16,400 feet.

[35] In Ross's time, the Earl of Minto was the First Lord of the Admiralty.

[36] *Polynya,* a Russian word, denotes an area of open water surrounded by ice—where ordinarily mineral-rich upwellings from the deep keep the surface open and nourish the plankton, which in turn attracts an abundance of vertebrate life. In the mid-seventies, a huge polyna that appeared in the Weddell Sea retained its mystery when it vanished once again a few years later.

[37] Only three ornithological groups have traveled here by icebreaker and none came so early, Werner tells us. A film crew for the excellent *Blue Planet* television series shown aboard ship came by chartered aircraft, having made special arrangements with the Italian research station at the south end of Terra Nova Bay.

[38] John Hay, *The Bird of Light,* Norton, 1993.

[39] See Frank Debenham's editorial footnote on this matter in the English edition of Bellingshausen's journals in Neider (p. 101); Debenham was an officer on Scott's *Terra Nova* expedition in 1911.

[40] Rex Hendry is on leave from his duties as chief ranger at New Zealand's Egmont National Park; Harry Keyes is a Kiwi mountaineer, volcanist, and glaciologist.

[41] Named for the Dundee whaler that was Scott's support ship on his 1901-1904 *Discovery* expedition and that became the main ship on the second expedition of 1911.

[42] German-born Antarctic explorer Erich von Drygalski was honored by Scott, whose *Discovery* expedition first reported the Ice Tongue's existence a century ago.

[43] "The eastern cape at the the foot of Mount Terror was named after my friend and colleague Commander Francis Rawdon Moira Crozier of the *Terror*" [Neider, *Antarctica,* 2001, p. 175]. Off what Ross called High Island, "a great number of whales were seen.... the larger kind having an extremely long erect back-fin while that of the smaller species was scarcely discernible" [Ross's journals quoted in Neider's, *Antarctica,* p. 194]— the orca and the minke.

[44] The glacier was named for manufacturer William Beardmore, his main sponsor.

[45] Shackleton reached 88° 23 minutes south latitude.

[46] Much of the polar exploration material is adapted from Roland Huntford's *The Last Place on Earth.*

[47] Icebergs are named for the quadrant of their origin: "A" from 0 to 90W (W. Weddell, etc.); "B" from 90 to 180W (Amundsen Land + E. Ross Sea); "C" from 180 to 90 E (W. Ross Sea + Wilkes Land); "D" from 90E to 0 (E. Weddell).

[48] The glacier is named for Prof. Edgeworth David of Shackleton's *Nimrod* expedition, who with geologists Douglas Mawson and Alistair MacKay were the first men to climb Mount Erebus, in 1908. The 51-year-old Dr. David, who described Mawson as "an Australian Nansen," was also a geologist on Mawson's Australasian Antarctic Expedition of 1911-14, which explored and mapped the unknown regions west of the Ross Sea and located the south magnetic pole.

[49] Lord Melbourne was British Prime Minister in Ross's time.

[50] *Antarctica,* 2001, p. 33.

[51] Told that an Auckland harbor was called Sarah's Bosom, Ross changed that wistful name to Erebus and Terror Harbor (now Ross Harbor) to honor the beloved dogs that accompanied him to the Antarctic.

[52] *Science Times,* March 2002.

[53] Robert McCormick, surgeon on the *Erebus,* in notes included in *A Voyage of Discovery and Research in the Southern and Antarctic Regions during the years 1839-43,* by Sir James Clark Ross.

[54] Viscount Adare, member of Parliament for Glamorganshire.

[55] As early as 1820, sealers in the South Shetland Islands were occasionally stranded by shipwreck and condemned to overwinter; also De Gerlache, Amundsen, Dr. Frederick Cook, and their unlucky shipmates passed more than a year (March 2, 1898, to March 14, 1899) on the icebound *Belgica,* drifting around the Bellingshausen Sea.

[56] Hansen's notes, turned over to the British Museum, would be studied by Edward Wilson before his own visit here in 1902 in the course of Scott's *Discovery* expedition.

[57] E. A. Wilson, *Diaries of Discovery and Terra Nova Expeditions,* Blandford Press, London, 1966, 1972. Excerpts from Wilson's journals, with many of his lovely sketches and paintings, may be found in *The Birds of Antarctica.*

[58] Rachel Tenni of Tasmania and Andrea Moser and Elke Fraider of Austria.

[59] Fridtjof Nansen, quoted in *Ninety Degrees North.*

[60] Notably Sir Edward Barrow of the RGS: see *Barrow's Boys*, Fergus Fleming, Atlantic Monthly Press, New York, 1948.

[61] Having said that, I invite the reader to critique the author's own unqualified reflections on the Antarctic explorers, to be found in the appendix.

[62] Somewhere in the Southern Ocean, according to U.S. satellite information, waves reach an average height of 36 feet every few days; Russian wave maps indicate maximum heights of 80 feet to 100 feet near the Kerguélens.

[63] Named for Charles Enderby and Sons, the British shipping firm whose tea was tossed into Boston Harbor at the start of the American Revolution; it was later a whaling company that sent out such eminent captains as John Balleny.

EPILOGUE

[1] Much of the historic material in the appendix is drawn from Roland Huntford's comprehensive work.

[2] *Antarctica*, 2001, pp. 512-13.

[3] See "Survival of the Hunter," *The New Yorker*, April 24, 1995.

[4] Huntford, pp. 205-207.

[5] Huntford, p. 207.

[6] Neider, pp. 210 and 215; also *Antarctica*, 2001, pp. 448-57.

[7] Huntford, p. 541.

[8] *Antarctica*, p. 457.

[9] The first men to stand at the North Pole were probably the crew of a Soviet air expedition on April 23, 1948. The first overland expedition to the South Pole after the Scott party would not turn up until January 1958, when teams led by Sir Vivian Fuchs and Sir Edmund Hillary drove up in tractors: Hillary also took four tractors on the first overland visit to Cape Crozier since The Worst Journey a half century before.

[10] Dr. Huntford strains to put the worst possible interpretation on Scott's every act; he makes the same points over and over, kicking his victim as hard as possible whenever he has him down.

[11] Scott's journals, quoted in *Birds*, p. 25.

[12] The writer Alan Villiers, who accompanied that voyage, quoted in *The Crystal Desert*, p. 222.

[13] *Antarctica*, p. 199.

[14] *Antarctica*, p. 199.

[15] Mawson's journals, quoted in *Antarctica*, 2001, pp. 460-65.

[16] Listed in *Who's Who* as discoverer of the South Magnetic Pole in East Antarctica during the *Nimrod* expedition, Mawson would later have his name removed when it was found that his measurements, taken in extreme conditions, had been slightly off.

BIBLIOGRAPHY

Antarctic reading over many years has led me to many useful books, a number of them referred to in this text, but a few have proved exceptionally useful:

Oceanic Birds of South America.(2 vol.), Robert C. Murphy. 1936.

The Worst Journey in the World. Apsley Cherry-Garrard. Chatto & Windus, London, 1952, 1st 1-vol edition, edit. with new introduction.

The Crystal Desert. David G. Campbell. Houghton Mifflin, Boston, Massachusetts, 1992.

The Last Place on Earth. Roland Huntford. Modern Library, New York, 1999.

Antarctica. McGonigal and Woodworth. Five Mile Press, Victoria, Australia, 2001.

Birds of the Antarctic. Edward Wilson. Humanities Press, New York, 1968.

Cherry. Sara Wheeler. Random House, New York, 2002.

The Endurance. Caroline Alexander. Knopf, New York, 1999.

Man and the Conquest of the Poles. Paul-Émile Victor. Simon and Schuster, New York, 1963.

Penguins: Past and Present, Here and There. George Gaylord Simpson. Yale University Press, New Haven, Connecticut, 1976.

Penguin Planet. Kevin Schafer. Northword Press, Minnetonka, Minnesota, 2000.

Antarctica: First Hand Accounts of Exploration and Endurance. Charles Neider, Cooper Square Press, New York, 1972.

Antarctica: A Guide to the Wildlife. Tony Soper. Globe Pequot Press, Guilford, Connecticut, 1994.

Among Whales. Roger Payne. Scribner, 1995.

Seals and Sirenians. R. Reeves, B. Stewart, S. Leatherwood. Sierra Club Books, San Francisco, California, 1992.

Tom Crean. Michael Smith. The Mountaineers Books, Seattle, Washington, 2000.

To this short list I would add the stirring journals of the various explorers, from Captain James Cook to Sir Ernest Shackleton. Some of these are excerpted in Charles Neider's useful *Antarctica: First Hand Accounts of Exploration and Endurance*, Cooper Square Press, New York, 1972, and others are available in reprints published by the Hakluyt Society in London.

Journal of the Resolution's Voyage in 1772, 1773, 1774, and 1775 on Discovery to the Southern Hemisphere by which The NON-EXISTENCE of an undiscovered CONTINENT, between the Equator and the 50th Degree of Southern Latitude, is demonstratively proved. John Marra, ed. 1775. Printed by F. Newbery, at the Corner of St. Paul's Churchyard.

A Voyage Round the World in his Britannic Majesty's Sloop, Resolution, Commanded by Captain James Cook, During the Years 1772, 3, 4, and 5. George Forster, London, 1775.

A Voyage Toward the South Pole, and Round the World. James Cook. London, 1777.

The Journals of Captain James Cook in His Voyages of Discovery (Edited from the Original Manuscripts by J. C. Beaglehole). Hakluyt Society, London, 1974.

The Resolution Jounal of Johann Reinhold Forster (1772-1775), vol. IV. Michael Hoare, ed. Hakluyt Society, London, 1982.

The Voyage of Captain Bellingshausen to the Antarctic Seas, 1819-1921. Frank Debenham, ed. London, 1945.

A Voyage Toward the South Pole. James Weddell. London, 1825.

Narrative of the United States Exploring Expedition. Charles Wilkes. Philadelphia, 1845.

A Voyage of Discovery and Research in the Southern and Antarctic Regions during the years 1839-43. James Clark Ross. London, 1847.

The Voyage of the "Discovery." Capt. R. F. Scott. London, 1905.

Scott's Last Expedition. Capt. R. F. Scott. London, 1913.

The South Pole. Roald Amundsen. London and New York, 1913.

South. Ernest Shackleton. New York, 1920.

INDEX

ACKNOWLEDGMENTS

Most of all, I wish to thank Birgit F. Bateman, for her generosity in permitting me to use some of her photographs of our Antarctic expeditions for this book, all the more so since these are used primarily as illustration and are not a fair representation of her fine work.

I should also like to thank my editors, in particular my excellent and generous friend, host, and fishing buddy Steve Byers, but also the admirable Ms. Johnna Rizzo, who has dealt most ably and cheerfully with the final drafts.